THE POWER WITHIN

THE POWER WITHIN

My Experience with the Holy Spirit

DAWN KELLUM

CONTENTS

To my Dad, Bishop Nathaniel Edwards, Sr., my Mom Lady Diane Edwards & my SisterMama Minister Natalie James

...'til we dance together again on the streets of gold

The Power Within
Copyright © 2021 by Dawn Kellum

First Printing, 2021

EISBN
978-0-578-85612-4
ISBN
978-0-578-85610-0

Introduction

My name is Dawn Kellum, author of The Power Within: My Experience with the Holy Spirit.

Thank you for coming along with me on this journey to my witness of the Holy Spirit of God in my life. I believe that I was inspired by the Holy Spirit of my Heavenly Father to write this book.

This is a book about how, as I surrender to the leading of my loving Heavenly Father, His Holy Spirit leads, guides, teaches, comforts, reveals and so much more. Much of the content in this book was gathered from about 8 years of documented testimonies, recorded visions, daily words of encouragement, some posted articles from my blog womenunspotted.com and more.

You will read about my personal testimonials on how God made a way for me and my family; stories of deliverance, prophetic visions I received that manifested and how God reveals situations. The book also contains me and my sister-in-law's testimonials about seeing the afterlife, my personal reports of miraculous healings and recorded amazing divine interventions. You will also hear about a vision of me seeing my child I regretfully aborted many years ago who is now grown and in the presence of God.

There are parts in this book about the power of love and forgiveness, powerful yoke-breaking prayers, words of faith and hope and spiritual insight to encourage and inspire.

The book begins on the subject of surrendering to a loving Heavenly Father who has our best interest at heart. Then I expound on His greatness and abiding in His presence. I continue on this journey to write about reasons why I love Jesus. Onward, I talk about the promises of God and meditation on the belief that I am who God says I am. Progression continues to personal testimonials, miraculous occurrences, divine favor, spiritual insight and God's power to heal, deliver and reveal through His Holy Spirit.

Err on the side of caution as you proceed further to witness my prophetic visions where I document hearing God's voice speaking to me and feeling His presence. God has given me grace to deal with some of the toughest visions. I trust Him to take care of me no matter what I face or deal with.

As you continue through the book you may understand more about the importance of appreciating life, the power of love and forgiveness. Hang on as I continue to document accounts of grief and how the Holy Spirit sends comfort.

Come along on this journey to behold me and my sister-in-law's inspiring experiences of seeing the afterlife - where believers in Jesus Christ go after this life on earth is over. To be absent from the body is to be present with God.

As you charter through, I document peculiar, amazing, bizarre and funny incidents.

As we near the end of the book you are routed into powerful prayers, words of faith and hope as well as wisdom for the time we are in now because "The Bridegroom Cometh."

I invite you to activate the power within you through the Holy Spirit you receive from Jesus Christ.

The following lists scriptures about the Holy Spirit:
John 14:26 ESV
But the Helper, the Holy Spirit, whom the Father will send in my name, he will teach you all things and bring to your remembrance all that I have said to you.

Acts 1:8 ESV
But you will receive power when the Holy Spirit has come upon you, and you will be my witnesses in Jerusalem and in all Judea and Samaria, and to the end of the earth."

Acts 2:38 ESV

And Peter said to them, "Repent and be baptized every one of you in the name of Jesus Christ for the forgiveness of your sins, and you will receive the gift of the Holy Spirit.

John 16:13 ESV

When the Spirit of truth comes, he will guide you into all the truth, for he will not speak on his own authority, but whatever he hears he will speak, and he will declare to you the things that are to come.

Romans 8:26-27 ESV

Likewise the Spirit helps us in our weakness. For we do not know what to pray for as we ought, but the Spirit himself intercedes for us with groanings too deep for words. And he who searches hearts knows what is the mind of the Spirit, because the Spirit intercedes for the saints according to the will of God.

Thank you again for taking this journey with me. I hope you are inspired.

CHAPTER 1

My Choice to Surrender to a Loving Father

You, as a sinner, are in a bad condition and God has the remedy. Rom. 3:23; Psalms 51; John 3:16 Recognize that Jesus Christ, the son of God, is the deliverer. All spirits – whether on earth and/or in Heaven must bow down to Jesus Christ, the son of God. Jesus has given us everything we need to be delivered.

Sin separates us from a good relationship with God. The penalty of sin is eternal damnation. In order to have a good relationship with God, Jesus Christ, the son of God and also the deliverer, gave his life in our (all human beings) stead on the cross of Calvary over 2000 years ago so every human being can be saved from eternal damnation if we receive Him as our Lord and Savior.

Romans 3:23 states "For all have sinned, and come short of the glory of God so all human beings need to receive Jesus Christ as their Lord and Savior in order to be saved from eternal torment/damnation and get power to live free from sinning or transgressing God's laws and commandments and/or being tormented by demons, evil spirits, Spirit Spouses, Incubus, Succubus, Sleep Paralysis and so much more. I John1:9 states If we confess our sins, he is faithful and just to forgive us our sins, and to cleanse us from all unrighteousness.

Pray the following prayer out loud:

"Father, in the name of thy son Jesus Christ, I know that I have broken your laws and my sins have separated me from you. I am truly sorry and now I want to repent and turn away from my past sinful life toward you. Please forgive me of all of my sins and help me avoid sinning again. I believe that your son Jesus Christ died for my sins and was resurrected from the dead, is alive, and hears my prayer. I invite Jesus Christ to become the Lord of my life and to rule and reign in my heart from this day forward. Please send your Holy Spirit or Holy Ghost to help me stop sinning and to obey you and to do Your will for the rest of my life In Jesus Christ name I pray. Amen."

-BAPTISM THROUGH WATER IN THE NAME OF JESUS. Be baptized (in water) for the forgiveness of sins (Acts 2:37-41; 1Peter 3:21; John 3:3-5; Acts 22:16; Romans 6:3-8; Colossians 2:12; Galatians 3:26-27; Mark 16:15-16; Acts 8:34-39; Titus 3:5; Ephesians 4:5; Matthew 28:18-20)

-BAPTISM BY THE HOLY SPIRIT. Remain faithful to Jesus Christ for the rest of our lives (Revelation 2:10; Matthew 24:13; Luke In order to REMAIN faithful and live overcoming lives, we strive to develop and form CHRIST WITHIN US by receiving the Holy Spirit aka Holy Ghost. Acts 2:1-39 Romans 8:9 – But ye are not in the flesh, but in the Spirit, if so be that the Spirit of God dwell in you. Now if any man have not the Spirit of Christ, he is none of his.

Submission to the Lord's will

Jesus Christ we surrender every desire that we have into Your hands and we trust in You for the outcome. We lay down our will for Your ultimate and perfect will in Jesus Name. We lay down our lives for Your glory; let us glorify Your Holy Name and let Your presence be ever before us in Jesus Name. We seek to honor You and glorify You Jesus Christ. Let us be pursuers of Your heart in Jesus Name. We desire to be fixed, focused and determined to follow after You Jesus Christ. We desire to be filled to overflowing in Your word. Let us not just be hearers of Your word; but doers of Your word.

Let us crave and hunger for Your word and for the deeper things of God. Let Your word be a seal upon our hearts and minds. Let us meditate on Your word and think on Your principles and precepts in Jesus Name. We desire You. You are more than enough for us. Your grace is more than enough. We praise You and glorify You in Jesus Name. God, be glorified in the name of Jesus Christ. Let our lives be honoring and glorifying to You in Jesus Name. Amen.

Oct 28, 2018, 7:39 AM

Dawn Kellum is feeling peaceful.
Meditation Moment:
II Corinthians 6:16 And what agreement hath the temple

of God with idols? For ye are the temple of the living God; as God hath said, I will dwell in them, and walk in them; and I will be their God, and they shall be my people.

17 Wherefore come out from among them, and be ye separate, saith the Lord, and touch not the unclean thing; and I will receive you,

18 And will be a Father unto you, and ye shall be my sons and daughters, saith the Lord Almighty.

Aug 29, 2020, 8:19 AM

Lord, you will grant us peace; all we have accomplished is really from you.

O Lord our God, others have ruled us, but you alone are the one we worship. Isaiah 26:12-13 (NLT)

May 19, 2015, 7:28 PM

Though heavy with the weight of my mistakes, You carried me and refused to let me sink under the pressure. You meant for me to soar. I am Your child and I'm worth fighting for. -"Worth Fighting For" - Brian Wilson

Apr 12, 2016, 10:42 PM

...if God don't give me the desires of my heart or ever deliver me, I know He is able and I still love Him. By His grace I will still remain faithful to Him and trust Him C O M P L E T E L Y.

Oct 13, 2015, 6:52 PM

Consistent faith and NO doubt in GOD and His word VS

doubt and NO consistent faith in anything other than GOD and His word.

Jun 13, 2015, 8:21 AM

My friend posted this inspirational analogy. Beautiful Trees.

When you look at trees, their branches are lifted up towards heaven. Even when the wind blows or storms are raging, trees still hold their place.

Even when a tree falls, its branches still try to stay in a Praise State. They're created to praise God the way they do and nothing will stop their obedience. The highest form of praise is obedience. Take it from the trees because they praise Him all day everyday. The trees can truly say praise is what they do.

Aug 16, 2015, 8:58 AM

Word of Caution: Stop seeking satisfaction from the affirmation and approval of people. Riches will also NOT fulfill you. The empty places in our hearts were created to be filled by God alone. The deepest thirst of our souls can only be quenched by God. Fill Me Up GOD.

Dec 30, 2015, 6:09 AM

No matter how large. No matter how small. God loves you. This reminds me of the song by the Canton Spirituals.

Apr 15, 2016, 8:20 PM

Dawn Kellum was watching God move on my behalf. Thank you Heavenly Father for protecting me and looking after me when I didn't have the strength to protect and/or look out for myself.

Apr 29, 2016, 12:27 PM

What is worth going to Hell's Torment over? Nothing. Nobody.

Every human being has an eternal soul. What does it profit you to gain the whole world, its riches, its things, all life's pleasures and more and lose your soul?

Remember that the time you spend on earth is less than 0% of eternity. What will you give in exchange for your soul? God forbids that you continue sinning and living in sin so that He can keep forgiving you? Every time you sin you are crucifying Christ Jesus all over again.

What is Salvation? The definition of salvation is "the deliverance, by the grace of God, FROM eternal punishment for sin which is granted to those who accept by faith God's conditions of repentance and faith in the Lord Jesus." Salvation is available in Jesus alone (John 14:6; Acts 4:12).

Truth About Salvation

1st Truth about Salvation: Being saved or receiving salvation through Jesus Christ is required for eternal life (eternally living) with God.

2nd Truth about Salvation: Being UNSAVED or NOT receiving salvation through Jesus Christ is the way to receive eternal damnation, eternal death or forever-dying and an eternal (forever) state of being separated from the grace of God.

Feb 3, 2018, 3:15 PM

...helping my babies with their homework and my 5-year old just told my 8-year old, "I hate my heart." My 8-year old responded "God took a piece of His heart and put it in yours so you can't hate your heart." WHOA! That one inspired me!!

May 23, 2016, 6:01 PM

Some people just have a problem being physically covered, mentally covered, emotionally covered, spiritually covered and overall covered. Covering is not always meant to restrict you, but to bless you. There's a blessing in the covering. Why let it all hang out while letting the good times roll on the highway to hell?

Jul 26, 2017, 12:09 PM

Do we want God to reign over us or someone else who would enslave us?

Aug 9, 2017, 9:09 PM

..the preacher preached ...And the evil spirit answered and said, Jesus I know [the authority He represents], and Paul I know [the authority backing Him]; but who are ye [what authority is backing you]? -Acts 19:15. You can never have God-Authority if you never submit to God's Authority. Has God given you permission to use His power to raise the dead, cast out demons, heal the sick, cleanse the lepers, give sight to the blind man, heal those with the palsy, etc?

Don't become so paralyzed by your giants that you're not allowing God to use you. We're created by God. It's not about us only. No. What you're going through is something bigger than you. You must overcome. Jesus Christ wants to be Lord of our lives and help us to overcome our giants. Somebody is waiting on us to overcome. Somebody is waiting for you to overcome.

Remember thy Creator in the days of thy youth. God allows our youthful years to be used as a leadership training for our future. Serve God with all your heart, mind, soul and strength. Put your hands in the hand of God and he will flip the script. Trust that God will turn things around for you. He will give you power to overcome your giant. He whom the Son of God, Jesus Christ, has set free is free indeed. I was bound but he set me free.

If you are bound by giants, Jesus knows how to make you free. Freedom come for me. God will give you power to overcome giants like abandonment, depression, abuse, rejection, bullying, broken relationships, addiction, fear, past failures and more. Saul was a king who was disobedient and not spiritual and allowed his giants to overcome him. David was a king who was obedient and righteous and overcame his giants. David used the armor that God had given him to defeat his giant Goliath.

Use what God gave you to defeat your giants. God knows what it takes to defeat your giants. Others need you to stand up in Kingdom of God authority like the men of Israel and Judah needed David to overcome the Philistine Goliath. You are in the Kingdom of God. Know who you are. Live so God's spirit will rest on you. Holy Spirit rest on me. Jesus said, "My Father and I will come and sup with you."

Nov 6, 2017, 7:13 AM

It doesn't take much for God to humble me because I HUMBLE MYSELF under the mighty hand of God.

Jun 15, 2020, 10:03 AM

What if you knew you were about to die? Are you ready to meet God? Are you in a position where you are ready to meet God?

Sep 6, 2020, 5:19 AM

Seriously. Are you ready to meet God? Let the pride go. Repent. Please repent. Jesus Christ is the way.

Sep 6, 2020, 5:48 AM

It doesn't matter how lonely you feel, don't seek comfort from ungodly spirits. They only want to kill, steal and destroy you and make you look like a traitor in the eyes of God. Get delivered!

Sep 24, 2020, 6:49 AM

Words that bring me peace: When you are a child of God and have given your life to Jesus Christ, no matter what evil comes your way, it ALWAYS ONLY works out for your good because you love God and your intents are to build up His Kingdom. Furthermore, when you surrender to God's will in your life & the favor of God is steering your life, nobody, no principality or power can move you from that position even if it's something you THINK you need.

God wants you to know that HE is the one and true God. It is HE who loves you the most & will not allow any other power to be god over you. God is more than the world against you dear hearts. No weapon formed against you shall be able to prosper. There is no power higher than God. The enemy is only allowed what God allows him for a reason.

This reminds me of the song "He is jealous for me. His love is like a hurricane. I'm like a tree. Oh how He loves us. Oh. Oh. How He loves us."

Apr 24, 2018, 6:52 AM

What are we putting in our bodies Spiritually?? What are we eating? Are we sitting at the table of the Lord, and yet, are we sitting at the table of the devil? Are we claiming we are Christians, yet, we are into things that are offensive to God? What are we reading? Watching, on television? Studying? Are they satanic? Are they evil? Are they adulterous? Do they mock God, and you accept it? Are they vampire movies, or movies about witches? Calling evil good?

All I know, is this, is that Christ, told us, he was the bread of Life. And for us to in remembrance, take the bread, take the wine, that represented His blood and life, and to live life holy. His body, broken for us, became the way, for redemption. He took the curse for us, because He had no sin.

So then with that comes great responsibility on our part; to be aware not to mix doctrine, accept hybrid doctrines of compromise that are filled with blasphemy, not to hate, not to take vengeance. Are you giving the devil a lot of attention? Are you taking your eyes off of Christ and just seeing the devil do things? Are you aware that God is the King of Kings, and has power, to heal you, bless you and change you? God created the heavens and the earth. Are you letting the devil deceive you? We cannot say we are Christians and act like the devil. Neither give any place to the devil. If you let him ride, he will take over and drive to enslave you. The sacrifice of Christ was too great for us to treat His death and life as shabby, mediocre or unworthy of our love.

Mar 21, 2019, 7:17 AM

My Dad taught me how to bless houses; but, a heart not surrendered to Jesus Christ can cause a blessed dwelling to turn into a dwelling where nobody wants to live.

May 8, 2019, 6:19 AM

CHAPTER 2

How Great is our God

Dawn Kellum updated her status.

Isaiah 41:10 Fear not, for I am with you; be not dismayed, for I am your God; I will strengthen you, I will help you, I will uphold you with my righteous right hand.

May 25, 2015, 7:37 PM

God spoke His word and brought the cosmos into existence. He made the universe. God is the most ingenious one. Humans at the pinnacle of their genius will NEVER approach the genius of God - W.U.M (Women Unspotted Ministries)

Jun 14, 2014, 8:32 AM

Dawn Kellum is feeling inspired.

Tell the 10 feet giant that God is bigger than him. Focus more on the big God than that problem that seems bigger than God. "When I fix my eyes on all that you are then every doubt I feel deep in my heart grows strangely dim"

Aug 3, 2014, 7:01 PM

God is not a statue that we can make and mold to our liking. God is everlasting to everlasting and exists always. God is like the potter. We are like the clay. God is not the clay to be formed to your liking. We are the temporary human beings that try to control the eternal God.

Dec 16, 2014, 8:05 PM

Dawn Kellum shared a memory.

Sisters and Brothers in Christ, The devil may be watching you and working full-time around the clock to discourage, destroy and sift you as wheat; but, God is in control of all things, including time, and is also working in your past, present and future at the SAME time to encourage you, build you up and give you VICTORY. Can The Church Say Amen.

Aug 20, 2016, 7:02 AM

Fear not [there is nothing to fear], for I am with you; do not look around you in terror and be dismayed, for I am your God. I will strengthen and harden you to difficulties, yes, I will help you; yes, I will hold you up and retain you with My [victorious] right hand of rightness and justice. For I the Lord your God hold your right hand; I am the Lord, Who says to you, Fear not; I will help you! - Isaiah 41:10, 13 (AMP)

Jul 23, 2015, 5:39 AM

HALLELUJAH is the same all over the world - a universal language. Praise God our Creator! Sing praises unto the God of our salvation.

Dec 5, 2013, 9:52 PM

We are little people in a small world, the footstool of the Great, Big, Omnipotent, Invisible, Omnipresent, Sovereign and Holy One.

May 6, 2019, 6:27 AM

Worship God everyday not just with your mouths with vain worship, but with pure worship and a sincere mind. Live holy. Don't be lukewarm. Worship requires humility, meditation and a deep understanding of how valuable God is.

Oct 20, 2018, 7:44 AM

He is the light in you and with you through the storm and at the end of the storm. Walk on. You'll never walk alone. Greater is He that is in you than He that is in the world. He is the great God, the God of Elijah and the God who is Jehovah Nissi.

Jan 9, 2019, 4:49 AM

One of the challenges we face as humans is sensing God's presence and knowing He is there. God is SO smart that He can allow us to sense him physically through the touch of a flower that He allowed to grow so intricately, through viewing the billions of living creatures on this earth and beyond that He provides life and more to, through the smell of the oceans that he created, through the taste of water after a drought, and through His touch that allows our bodies to be healed. God is real!

Apr 19, 2013, 9:23 PM

Questions. Questions. If God knew us before we were born, where were we?

May 21, 2013, 1:50 AM

Questions! Questions! SCENARIO - for example....What if you created your own world? Let's say you ONLY created that world based off of 1 percent of your knowledge. Therefore, anything in that world could ONLY attain to that 1 percent of the Creator's knowledge because that is all that you ALLOWED it to know....HOW GREAT IS GOD???????? Do you know??? God surpasses ALL human knowledge and our cognizance. God is omniscient or all-knowing...He knows more than you could ever imagine...

May 21, 2013, 1:59 AM

CHAPTER 3

In His Presence

I can BOLDLY say, The Lord is my helper, and I will NOT fear what man shall do unto me. - Hebrews 13:6

Aug 12, 2014, 6:21 PM

Praise God in spite of how you feel...

Mar 8, 2014, 3:46 PM

There is power in the blood of Jesus Christ. You cannot use the blood of Jesus Christ until it is inside you; this happens when you are born again and receive salvation through Jesus Christ. THEN the blood of Jesus Christ is to be used by you against all the powers of the devil, against all envy, strife, hate and sin. Use the blood of Jesus Christ against every unclean spirit and unclean thought that tries to leech your mind.

Thoughts that can destroy the anointing of God in your life will come, but the blood will help you to not embrace them, to not endorse them, to not hold onto them. - Ernest Angley

Apr 12, 2014, 5:16 AM

Are you aware of His presence? He is joy in sorrow, peace in the storm, strength through the weaknesses and praise in the time of heaviness. The blessings of the Lord maketh RICH and addeth NO sorrow.

Jun 12, 2014, 8:18 PM

Dawn Kellum updated her status.

I feel the presence of God much stronger when my heart breaks from the SAME things that break His heart. His desire is that all humanity be saved, healed, delivered, spend eternity with Him in peace and MUCH more. Those should be our desires as well as people of God.

We should not get it twisted. We THINK we KNOW a better way outside of God's way; but, we don't. We are only mere TEMPORARY human beings who still only know very LITTLE about the only true and living GOD that ALWAYS existed and from whom we all came from. Father Knows BEST.

Nov 1, 2014, 8:21 AM

Lord prepare me to be a sanctuary pure and holy, tried and true and, with thanksgiving, I'll be a living sanctuary for you. Sanctify me. I want My Body To Be A Home For God.

Apr 29, 2015, 6:49 AM

Meditating: The things I don't see with my physical eyes are eternal. The things I see with my physical eyes are temporal, so, in order to believe that the eternal things exist, I must use faith to see them and not through my physical eyes.

Mar 9, 2015, 6:10 PM

Dawn Kellum updated her status.

Blessed is the person who does not follow the advice of wicked people, take the path of sinners, or join the company of mockers. Rather, he delights in the teachings of the Lord and reflects on his teachings day and night. Psalms 1:1-2 (GW)

Oct 7, 2015, 5:39 PM

Dawn Kellum wrote on Women Unspotted Ministries' timeline.

But let all those that put their trust in thee rejoice: let them ever shout for joy, because thou defendest them: let them also that love thy name be joyful in thee. Psalms 5:11

Jun 1, 2015, 12:42 AM

It is amazing to see how fears are overcome when you simply relax and trust God. I thank God for peace.

Aug 24, 2015, 5:09 AM

God is Faithful
Updated Jul 15, 2015, 11:55 PM
Jul 15, 2015, 11:55 PM

Dawn Kellum was at Apostolic Tower of Power Temple.

Come on praise team. I got more strength now. Let's continue to praise Him for a few more hours. "Higher...Higher. Lift Jesus. Higher...Higher" Daddy, play that bass guitar. De'ja, play that keyboard. Justin and William, play those

drums. Let us ALL sing and praise the name of the Lord. Everybody glorify Him "Higher...Higher...Higher."
Oct 11, 2015, 10:16 PM

Word of Wisdom: Rid yourself of negative thoughts by listening to worship music unto God. Don't turn it off until the good thoughts come. It works.
Nov 19, 2015, 12:56 PM

The anointing makes all the difference. I was singing at my Dad's church last night. I asked the Lord what to sing. He told me what to sing so I sung just that. After church someone came up to me and said, "I had a sharp pain radiating on the side of my body; but, when you sung it went away!!" Singers and Praisers sing and worship under God's anointing. It makes ALL the difference.
Oct 26, 2015, 6:53 AM

22 received the baptism of the Holy Spirit last night at the PCAF Holy Convocation AND a man who couldn't speak SPOKE!!! Praise God.
Jul 30, 2017, 8:12 AM

Many of my questions are answered as I keep my mind focused on helping the kingdom of God - not on riches, fame or fortune. There is less stress, less wasted time and less frustration. If any of you lack wisdom, let him ask of God, that giveth to all men liberally, and upbraideth not; and it shall be given him. Ref. James 1:5
Jun 4, 2016, 9:17 AM

Know who you are. Live so God's spirit will rest on you. Holy Spirit rest on me. Jesus said, "My Father and I will come and sup with you."

Jun 29, 2017, 6:18 AM

Here is something I shared with one of my babies yesterday when they asked me about the trinity. "Look at your fingers. Each has 3 sections just like the trinity. 1 - Father, 2 - Son 3 - Holy Spirit. All 3 sections are apart of 1 finger. They are all one and all connected and do not operate without the other. You see them on your hands to remind you of the relationship and that you are also connected to them. That's why God said, "Let us make man in our image and our likeness." They got it then.

Jul 31, 2017, 2:17 PM

Worthy Conversations:

Me: "Thank you God for another day. Thank you for [filled in personal information]. I enter your courts with praise and your gates with Thanksgiving. You alone are awesome in your ways and worthy of all my praise. You are greater than anyone and anything."

God: "How are you my child?"

Dec 22, 2017, 12:34 PM

Whatever you're focused on changes your purpose. How can you hear from God with all the noise and distractions in your life? We know how to fast from food and water but do we know how to fast from social media to hear from God and to stay focused on purpose? - inspired by Elder N. Singleton from Missionary Service

Oct 6, 2017, 5:20 AM

The preacher preached about the Power in God. When a person disconnects from God they start to spiritually die. God wants men to reach after him. God is not far from us. King Herod was trying to convince the people he had power over God. There is no power greater than God. The kingdom suffereth violence but the violent take it by force. Be anxious for nothing but pray and seek God. God will give you peace. Get your power out of the box and start using it - just as nuclear power is Unleashed, Unleash Your power that God has given you. Activate your power. Ask and you shall receive. God wants us to have joy. Seek and you shall find. God can fix situations and turn them around.

Oct 31, 2017, 7:32 AM

Whatever we, as believers and followers of Christ Jesus, go through in life, He has promised to never leave us or forsake us. He promised to be with us always. As we walk through the valley of the shadow of death we will fear no evil for He is with us. His rod and staff comforts us. Ref. Psalms 23. If we walk through the waters He will not allow us to drown if we trust in Him. God is with us. He is the only stable and faithful one in our lives. Only trust Him. Cling fast to and rely on Jesus Christ. He is Heaven to me.

Everything else that looks or may feel like heaven is a counterfeit. Trust God to the core that He will work the tough situations out His way. God has already bound the strong man and prepared a way for you to handle the tough situation in front of you. Consider the spies who spied out the land in Numbers chapter 13 and said that we are more than able to conquer them. Praise God like you know He has it all worked out. Have faith. Thank God for the mountains because, as long as Jesus is your friend, you have the victory. Deuteronomy chapter 8 verse 3 God suffered thee to hunger and fed thee with manna or angels' food. It's hard looking at a situation that is tough when you consider your own strength but with God all things are possible. If it is God's will, God has already gone before you to prepare your victory. The name of your situation is victory. Say, "I can do all things through Christ Jesus who strengthens me. Greater is He that is in me than he that is in the world." All things work out together for the good of them who love the Lord and to them called according to His purpose. Deuteronomy 9: 1 – 2; Deuteronomy 8:2 – 3; Deuteronomy 9:1 – 2; Deuteronomy 11:24; Philippians 4:13; Joshua 1:3 - 4

Dec 3, 2017, 8:05 AM

Philippians 4:8 ESV. Finally, brothers, whatever is true, whatever is honorable, whatever is just, whatever is pure, whatever is lovely, whatever is commendable, if there is any excellence, if there is anything worthy of praise, think about these things

Feb 22, 2019, 7:07 AM

Trust in God. Fear not. You are not alone. You are surrounded by angels on assignment who carry the glory of God.

They are walking with you at this moment and they have you covered on all sides.

Apr 6, 2020, 9:12 PM

One night with the King can change everything.

Dec 6, 2019, 8:58 AM

Sometimes the most tender and delicate flowers need to be placed in an environment where they can heal properly and grow stronger like a premature baby needs an incubator. Grow flower grow. Grow child of God grow.

Jul 9, 2019, 6:16 PM

Message to all of my fellow gospel and Christian singers and musicians: Worship is a lifestyle not a specific song or musical composition. We are worshippers who surrender our lives to God for His use and purpose; not just on Sundays or during church conventions. We are not part time lovers of God. We are believers in the Christian faith and live according to the gospel of Jesus Christ.

There is a demonic chord. Know what it is and never compose a Christian song with it or sing a song to God with it. You want God to be pleased to dwell in the midst of your praises unto Him. How would you like for someone to praise you on something and curse you at the same time? Keep a repentant heart always and live a life free from sin. If you sin, repent quickly and really be Godly sorry for your offense to His Holy Majesty.

Don't continue in sin so grace can abound. God forbids that. Stay prayerful always. Get rid of pride. Know that your gift(s) can be taken like mine was in 2015 with no notice. Gifts vs Anointing? Gifts and talents are given without repentance and without a good relationship with God. The anointing is different and not taught; but, only given by God. You can only minister under the anointing of God when you know and live the truth of God through His son Jesus Christ and surrendering your life to Him. The anointing breaks yokes, lifts heavy burdens, raises the dead, heals the sick, brings freedom to those held captive spiritually, casts away demons and evil spirits and so much more. The anointing is what the world needs now. 1 John 2:20 But you have an anointing from the Holy One, and all of you know the truth.

1 John 2:27 As for you, the anointing you received from him remains in you, and you do not need anyone to teach you. But as his anointing teaches you about all things and as that anointing is real, not counterfeit—just as it has taught you, remain in him.

Jul 13, 2019, 8:12 AM

Let your worship and praise to God shift the atmosphere
Aug 12, 2013, 6:16 PM

God dwells in the midst of praises. Something miraculous WILL happen when you praise Him from your heart...Glory to God
Jan 9, 2014, 11:21 PM

We can trust our God. He is WITH US Our hearts can safely trust in Him.
Feb 12, 2014, 9:45 PM

CHAPTER 4

Why Do I Love Jesus?

Dawn Kellum is feeling inspired.

I am a witness that God will work it out. Trust God. He transcends time and space and I just witnessed ANOTHER round of miracles that He can do ANYTHING if you ONLY trust Him. HE HOLDS MY HEART (TEARS OF JOY) Hallelujah!

Apr 5, 2014, 2:07 AM

Dawn Kellum is feeling blessed.

Romans 8:35-37 Can anything ever separate us from Christ's love? Does it mean he no longer loves us if we have trouble or calamity, or are persecuted, or hungry, or destitute, or in danger, or threatened with death? NO. Despite all these things, overwhelming victory is ours through Christ, who loved us.

May 12, 2015, 7:01 AM

Even if life gives you a thousand reasons to QUIT, God will give you a thousand and one more to keep going - Author Unknown

The thoughts that God thinks of us are MORE than the sands of the sea because He has MANY wonderful plans in store for those who love and know Him. Imagine 10 million years from now in eternity with God and NEVER getting bored. How about 12 million years or maybe 100 million years?

You see? You have MORE reasons to hang in there than YOU can EVEN imagine. Don't give up. Trust God.

Jun 7, 2014, 2:27 PM

Why do I love Jesus challenge. I was nominated by a friend.

I love Jesus because He taught me what real love is. I love Jesus because He became the scapegoat for my sins. I love Jesus because He carries the weight of sins of the whole world. I love Jesus because there is no life worth living outside of Him. I love Jesus because He has the keys to death, hell and the grave and He holds the key to my heart AND my destiny. I love Jesus because He never lied to me. I love Jesus because He really knows How to save anybody. I love Jesus because He saved me from the inside out. I love Jesus because only He understands me. I love Jesus because He has healed my body multiple times. I love Jesus because He has healed my children, family and loved ones multiple times. I love Jesus because He loved me unconditionally and MADE me feel worthy of His love when I didn't think I deserved His unfailing love. I love Jesus because I would not exist in Him if He didn't allow it. I love Jesus because He is the BEST thing that ever happened to me. I love Jesus because He is with me always even when I'm not always aware of His presence. I love Jesus because He is very real to me. I love Jesus because He is giving me the victory over circumstances by fighting my battles FOR me. I love Jesus because my van completely shut-off the other day while I was still driving it in the middle of traffic and He protected my 2 daughters and I from a potentially fatal accident. I love Jesus because He protected me and cared for me and loved me unconditionally when I fell from grace and betrayed His trust in me to never forsake Him.

Aug 30, 2014, 6:54 PM

Why do I love Jesus challenge. I was nominated by another friend.

I love Jesus because He is my Savior, and when the storms are raging, He is my shelter. When I'm grieving He is my comfort and when I'm down he protects my mind, and when I'm lost He gives me direction because He is Alpha and Omega, the beginning and the end and He ALWAYS knows the way. Where He leads me I will follow. I love Jesus because when I proclaim His promises, He honors every one. I love Jesus because he promised to be with me until the end of the age and He is with me. I love Him so. He is wonderful. I love Jesus because He is the Lord from Heaven. I love Jesus because he protects me as I sleep at night. I love Jesus because He is the ONLY one that truly understands the human condition and each individual. I love Jesus because He is the only one that knows the best for each and every one of us. I love Jesus because He has prepared many mansions in heaven for us so we will not be homeless when we get to Heaven. I love Jesus because if it hadn't been for Him always having my best interest at heart, I would have truly been consumed and currently burning in the flames of hell's torment. I love Jesus because

I know Him and how He works and there is something new and exciting to learn about Him every day. I love Jesus because He is taking good care of all of my loved ones who have passed on in Him. I love Jesus because He is taking good care of all of my little babies I lost and He so loves my offspring that He gave them a name even when I didn't have the opportunity to name them. He is so very loving. I love Jesus. I truly love Jesus. I love Jesus because even though He is the Lord from Heaven and worthy of eternal honor, He still considers me as one of His - little old me. I guess I am somebody because Jesus makes sure I AM somebody. I love Him so.

Aug 30, 2014, 6:55 PM

What I do for Christ is what eternally matters
Dec 22, 2014, 8:26 AM

Dawn Kellum is feeling loved.

Singing Jesus loves me this I know for the Bible tells me so and Love lifted me. Love lifted me. When nothing else could help love lifted me. The love of Jesus Christ conquers all. That is the Love which Conquers All.

May 3, 2015, 8:02 AM

Sisters and Brothers in Christ, the devil may be watching you and working full-time around the clock to discourage, destroy and sift you as wheat; but, God is in control of all things, including time, and is also working in your past, present and future at the SAME time to encourage you, build you up and give you VICTORY.

Aug 20, 2015, 5:48 AM

A Lady at the store: Hello. You have a very bright aura. Have you ever had a reading?

Me: No. Thank you. I have never done that before. (smiles)

Lady: You are smiling on the outside but very sad on the inside. You look strong on the outside but are very weak on the inside.

Me: That's why we need Jesus to help us along the way (smiles)

Lady: Yes. You are right. God bless you my sister. Have a blessed day

Me: Thank you (smiles)

Aug 11, 2015, 7:47 AM

Does it matter who stopped following you on Facebook when Christ Jesus is constantly pursuing you?

Jul 17, 2015, 5:04 AM

I love this. Through Jesus Christ was everything made that was made so He is the reason why we're alive and even able to celebrate anything.

Dec 23, 2017, 7:10 AM

Word of Caution: Being Ethical with this world's right-eousness alone or having good works does NOT or will NOT save us. Only Jesus Christ can save us. By grace are we saved and NOT by works just in case we want to boast.

Feb 19, 2016, 4:45 AM

Jesus Christ is the only way to the Father and to Heaven. I'm not interested in a satanic smörgåsbord

Feb 28, 2016, 7:34 PM

In my darkness I was trying to find that void that only Jesus Christ could fill. Who would have known that when the light came on He was right there pursuing me all along. He found me (Tears of joy).

Mar 8, 2016, 7:06 AM

I plan to help lead "I'd Do It Again" by Tasha Cobbs with my church choir. Jesus believed that YOU were worth Him giving His life up to be crucified brutally, marred more than ANY man and so much more. He loved us even when we hated Him.

Apr 7, 2016, 7:08 AM

Be not dismayed or discouraged. You are loved by Jesus Christ; the bishop of your soul, the comforter and the one who loves at all times. Trust Him. God bless you.

Apr 9, 2016, 2:52 PM

Jesus Christ has NOT betrayed us; but cherishes us and loves us. Why do we betray Him, refuse to cherish Him and refuse to love Him? Why do we refuse to live for Him?

Mar 11, 2017, 5:02 AM

Jesus Christ wants to eat with you vs satan who wants to devour (eat) you.

Sep 8, 2016, 5:35 AM

It's amazing to see how many of us spend money trying to impress people, make "friends" or get people to like us. Once we run out of money those "friends" run away and turn their back. What happened to the friends who just love you for you instead of loving your money or the stuff you got? I've learned in my 42 years of life on earth that Jesus Christ is the best friend anybody could EVER have. Some can't physically see Him but He is omnipresent, always working on your behalf and ALWAYS has your best interest at heart.

Oct 22, 2017, 8:38 AM

Dawn Kellum is feeling peaceful.

I belong to Jesus so I know He will take care of me; with the heart and faith of a child I will listen and do what He tells me. I know He loves me. I know He cares. I surrender all to Jesus my blessed Savior.

Sep 7, 2017, 7:07 AM

I will run to you. You are the healer and savior of my soul. I will run to you. No matter what happens. No matter how I feel. If I don't feel you near me, I will still run to you and call your name. I will sing praises unto your name. I will run to you.

Nov 12, 2017, 7:31 AM

Jesus said to her, "I am the resurrection and the life; he who believes in Me will live even if he dies,

For since by man came death, by man came also the resurrection of the dead. For as in Adam all die, even so in Christ shall all be made alive."

Dec 20, 2017, 5:57 AM

"I love Jesus. He is my savior. When the storms are raging He is my shelter. Where He leads me, I will follow. I love Jesus. He loves me." He is SO good to me and has NEVER lied to me.

Jun 28, 2013, 11:10 AM

Though heavy with the weight of my mistakes, you carried me and refused to let me sink under the pressure. You meant for me to soar. I am Your child and I'm worth fighting for. - "Worth Fighting For" by Brian Wilson

Apr 12, 2020, 10:20 AM

Do we know Him? Does He know us or does He say, "I used to know them, but I don't know them anymore?" No. He either knows you or He never knew you.

Jan 4, 2020, 5:45 AM

Merry Christmas 2019. Happy Birthday Jesus. The guest of honor lives in the hearts of all who love and know Him. He also sits in the real tabernacle and on the right hand of the Father. Through Him was made all things that was made. He has always existed and reigns forever. He is the rider upon the white horse and is called true and faithful. He defies all scientific explanations. He became the sacrifice for the sins of all humanity. The list goes on and on. Joy to the world the Lord has come. Let earth receive her king.

Dec 25, 2019, 11:27 PM

There is power in the blood of Jesus Christ. You cannot use the blood of Jesus Christ until it is inside you; this happens when you are born again and receive salvation through Jesus Christ. THEN the blood of Jesus Christ is to be used by you against all the powers of the devil, against all envy, strife, hate and sin. Use the blood of Jesus Christ against every unclean spirit and unclean thought that tries to leech your mind. Thoughts that can destroy the anointing of God in your life will come, but the blood will help you to not embrace them, to not endorse them, to not hold onto them. - Ernest Angley

Apr 12, 2020, 10:11 AM

"Simon, Simon, behold, Satan demanded to have you, that he might sift you like wheat, but I have prayed for you that your faith may not fail. And when you have turned again, strengthen your brothers."

Apr 18, 2020, 9:09 AM

Hebrews 4:15 For we do not have a High Priest who cannot sympathize with our weaknesses, but was in all points tempted as we are, yet without sin.

Jul 16, 2013, 9:07 PM

I am feeling heartbroken from things and people in this world and feeling loved by my Lord from Heaven - Jesus Christ to whom my heart does safely trusts in. Psalms 34:18. The Lord is close to those who are of a broken heart

Jul 5, 2013, 10:44 AM

Is Jesus Christ your BFF (Best Friend Forever)?
Jan 9, 2014, 11:24 PM

CHAPTER 5

God's Promises

Dawn Kellum is feeling peaceful.

I am thankful for the ability to rest in the finished outcome and knowing that at the end is victory

Nov 11, 2014, 3:00 AM

If my people, which are called by my name, shall humble themselves, and pray, and seek my face, and turn from their wicked ways; then will I hear from heaven, and will forgive their sin, and will heal their land. Ref. 2 Chronicles 7:14. Repent.

Sep 22, 2015, 10:30 PM

We can trust our God
He knows what He's doing
Though it might hurt now
He's holding on to you and me
And He's never gonna leave, No.
He is with us, He is with us
Always, always - "He is With Us" by Love and the Outcome

Jul 10, 2015, 3:25 AM

Question - Why does God have us wait?

Answer-To build your faith in a dungeon and during the valley in your life where it's too dark to see and too hard to believe.

Answer-To build your dependence on Him when you are barren and empty to see if He is truly all you desire and all you need.

Answer-To see how well you will trust and serve Him when you are still stuck in the background somewhere, doing "seemingly" nothing too significant for Him.

Answer - To build your trust in Him when the storm keeps raging, the battle keeps going and breakthrough and victory doesn't seem near.

GOAL- Grow in faith. Learn to only depend on God. -taken from The Praying Woman Facebook Page

Aug 4, 2017, 8:42 AM

Some people don't believe the whole plan of salvation through Jesus Christ, the second coming and more because they do not feel they are worthy enough of such great honor. Remember that Nobody is worthy of such great honor. But Jesus Christ thought that we were worth it. He made us worthy of such awesomeness. Believe.

Jan 30, 2017, 6:54 AM

In all of life's dilemmas, the bottom line is that we live on a promise: "God has said, 'Never will I leave you; never will I forsake you'" (Hebrews 13:5). Every believer needs to get to a place where that promise is enough.

Jul 11, 2017, 7:50 PM

Meditating: Stop sulking in self-pity. You are a child of God. If you want to experience unlimited miracles of God in your life this week, you must launch out on faith, keep the faith, surrender to His divine will and hold onto His promises by believing them and professing them. It is like an obedient pilot flying an airplane on autopilot while, once the airplane takes off, it stays steady even through severe turbulence which results in decreased speed and un-comfortability. ENDURE!

Luke 18:8 (KJV) I tell you that he will avenge them speedily. Nevertheless when the Son of man cometh, shall he find FAITH on the earth?

May 30, 2019, 10:45 AM

"We are given moral intuition by God. Have faith in God. Faith is deliberately choosing that God will do what He says." - Bishop Singleton on Sunday, May 12, 2019

May 18, 2019, 8:32 AM

Thankful Thursday: Through it all I'm standing on God's promises and inspired to make good choices even through this rough sea called Life. I will not be influenced by satan to make bad choices and give up my kingdom birthright like Esau did as well as other present believers have. Some things in this life don't feel good at all and sometimes I feel like giving up or throwing in the towel; but, I still love God. God certainly loves me and has a purpose for my pain. I am trusting God's process no matter how long the "night." I will praise God not only because He is working it all out for my good because I love Him; but, because He is the sovereign Lord and King of kings. Though He slay me, yet will I trust Him even through humiliation, sickness, uncertainty and the "night." If He never delivers me, I know He is still able; but, I must trust that my heavenly Father knows best.

"I love you Lord. I love you Lord. I love you Lord today because you cared for me in such a special way. I praise you and I lift you up and I magnify your name. That's why my heart is filled with praise." Praise Through Adversity because You Win through Jesus.

Aug 1, 2019, 6:35 AM

We ran out of one of the entrees to feed the children at one of my jobs today. I had already called headquarters to order more food. I was waiting patiently. Thankfully, the children had other entrees to choose from. Workers were panicking left and right. One worker, in particular, looked at me, as I was cutting grape vines to refill the nutrition bar with a smile on my face, and said, "Are you Ok?" I responded, "Yes, I'm in my happy place." He said, "Did you hear what the person just asked you?" I said, "Yes. I've already responded and said the food was ordered and it should be here." A few minutes later the delivery person comes in with the desired entrees and we all cheer.

Life Lesson Takeaway: You prayed for it and God promised you that thing. God will bring it to pass in its time which is not always your timing. Have peace even through the storm as you wait. Sometimes things get much worse before the promise comes - like a pregnancy or like when Jesus and the disciples were on the stormy sea before the man with many demons was delivered. You need to know that what you are waiting on is actually worth the wait. Be encouraged. God will give you peace in the storm and encourage your soul. Don't let the devil discourage you. Keep hope alive and stand firm on the promises of God. It's on the way.

Dec 5, 2019, 6:58 PM

Good Morning Family. Whatever God promised, He will fulfill it. Let us not run around hurting people and God's children because we are angry with God and don't understand His ways. Sometimes it takes us going through an unexpected season (hardship, situations forcing us to look straight to God for help, uncertainty, emotional damage, etc.) to yield the expected promises God has given. All things work out together for the good of them who love the Lord and those called according to His purpose. Every human being has value in God's eyes. Be patient. Let patience have her perfect work. Let God's will be done on earth as it is in Heaven.

Sep 11, 2019, 5:51 AM

Thirsty Thursdays: Who cares if they told you, "No." If God promised you something, it's coming. Keep believing and keep trusting God. If love believes that anything can happen, then our love for God believes that He can make anything happen. Go back to the ones who said, "No" like Moses did when Pharaoh said, "No. I will not let God's people out of bondage." Moses went back a few times. Let Heaven's cloud of witnesses look at you and rejoice that your faith is not failing because Jesus is praying that it won't. The promise is coming. I waited 7 years and endured 9 miscarriages before my 2nd child was born. Let God bring the promise in His time. His thoughts are higher than ours. Remember?

Sep 12, 2019, 7:18 AM

Sermon notes 092720 - Whatever we sow we shall reap. We shall reap more and longer than we sow.

It's time to sow the word of God in your life and to your spirit continually with a good heart. Sow to the spirit and reap life eternal. The word of God must be planted deep with broken up ground and not planted on the surface. Deeply planted word germinates to a desired effect. The seed of the word is not genetically modified but divinely modified and alive. The devil is like the thorns that try to choke the word out of you.

Stop letting the thorns take over. Let the divinely modified seed planted deep within you go through the process.

Sep 27, 2020, 3:50 PM

Proclaim the word of GOD through faith WHILE YOU WAIT on the promises of God until the word of GOD through faith REVEALS the promises of God in the physical. KEEP THE FAITH. God WILL do as He Promised.

Dec 2, 2013, 6:26 AM

I've been singing this song throughout the ENTIRE day today. "HOLD ON TO THE PROMISES. Hold tight." I love this song.

Dec 12, 2013, 5:55 PM

God, You said there is no temptation that has come to me or that can come to me that is not common to man, nothing that is beyond human resistance. You are faithful to Your Word and to Your love for me, and You will not allow me to be tempted beyond my strength to resist and You will provide a way out or a way of escape so I will be strong against it – 1 Corinthians 10:13. Be Encouraged.

Nov 13, 2013, 11:53 PM

CHAPTER 6

I Am Who God Says I Am

Repost from a friend: When I married my husband I proudly took on his name. I had a new name and a new identity - Mrs. Kellum. When I went down in the waters of baptism, I proudly took on the name of Jesus. I also had a new name and a new identity - the beloved of God. Don't forget who you are, and whose you are. Be proud to carry His name - Jesus. There's something about that name ya'll.

Apr 2, 2015, 6:28 PM

Dawn Kellum is feeling inspired.

Yesterday evening my 4-year old daughter walked past the toddler room at the gym - where she only visited maybe twice - and told her sister, "When I went there they called me a monster in there. I'm NOT a monster. I'm a child of God!"

Mar 17, 2015, 6:41 AM

The keeper of creation knows your name.

Apr 22, 2016, 6:01 AM

You are treasured. You are sacred. You are His. You're Beautiful. You're made for so much more than this. You're beautiful in the eyes of God. - Beautiful by Mercy Me
Mar 8, 2016, 9:19 PM

Happy 87th Birthday Bishop Singleton - a man of God with a heart of love for all people. One of my favorite sayings by him is "The people didn't hire me. God did!" God bless you Bishop.
Oct 18, 2015, 9:41 AM

To all my chain message senders: Please don't send me any more chain messages. I know I'm beautiful, a good mom, loved by God, blessed and much more because of God's grace NOT because YOU said it. I don't need anyone to validate any of that. My witness is in Heaven and my record is on high. God's opinion of me matters the very most - not yours. Good Day!
Oct 19, 2017, 7:44 AM

Know that you are LOVED*
Know that you are Outstanding
Know that you are Valuable
Know that you Exist
Know that you Deserve time and space...
.......And this world would not be the same without you. GOD loves YOU with an "unchanging" love. Your friends and family need you . You are so important. Just know.
Jun 8, 2018, 10:27 PM

Everybody has value and a purpose in this life. God told Jeremiah, the "Weeping Eyed" prophet, "I knew you before I formed you in your mother's womb." Although some of us got here through horrible means like rape, incest, etc., we are still greatly valued and have PURPOSE. Live your best life in Jesus name.

Sep 12, 2019, 7:24 AM

As a follower of Christ Jesus

I am a fellow citizen with the rest of God's family (Eph. 2:19)

I am righteous and holy (Eph. 4:24)

I am a citizen of heaven, seated in heaven right now (Eph. 2:6; Phil. 3:20)

I am hidden with Christ in God (Col. 3:3)

I am an expression of the life of Christ because He is my life (Col. 3:4)

I am chosen of God, holy and dearly loved (Col. 3:12; I Thess. 1:4)

I am a son/daughter of light and not of darkness (I Thess. 5:5)

I am a holy partaker of a heavenly calling (Heb. 3:1)

I am a partaker of Christ; I share in His life (Heb. 3:14)

I am one of God's living stones, being built up in Christ as a spiritual house (I Pet. 2:5)

I am a member of a chosen race, a royal priesthood, a holy nation, a people for God's own possession (I Pet. 2:9,10)

I am an enemy of the devil (I Pet. 5:8)

I am a child of God and I will resemble Christ when He returns (I John 3:1,2)

I am born of God, and the evil one – the devil – cannot touch me (I John 5:18)

I am NOT the great "I am" (Exod. 3:14; John 8:24, 28, 58), but by the grace of God, I am what I am (I Cor. 15:10)

Oct 28, 2018, 7:34 PM

My human intuition can sense a higher power much stronger, smarter, much wiser, more alert, much better, much tougher and more perfect than myself looking out for me. My faith believes this is Jesus Christ my Lord who always has my best interest at heart. Lead me oh my great Messiah who is true, faithful and righteous through your Holy Spirit. You are my Mediator, good master, ruler, the keeper of my soul and the one who answers prayer. I surrender all to you my blessed Savior. You are my mind regulator; The lion of the tribe of Judah who will never lie to you; The good Shepherd King of Kings healer comforter I know Him. Do you know Him? My relationship with Him is me solely depending on Him in EVERY area of my life, me spending time in worship to Him, me learning about Him, me wanting to spend eternity with Him. He is my good Master who loves me.

Feb 2, 2018, 7:30 AM

...me with the love of Jesus Christ in my heart and the peace of God. [My first name is Dawn. My middle name is Hope.] [As long as I am alive I will have Hope.] But still, like air, I'll rise. But still, like dust, I'll rise. Just like hopes springing high,

Still I'll rise. I am the dream and the hope of the slave. I rise [continually]. I rise [so those who are bound in the now may rise]. I rise [so my ancestors prayers are answered while they rest with God]. [GOD please help me to rise, my loved ones to rise, my babies to rise, my friends to rise...] I was made on purpose for purpose. We are His workmanship. Everything belongs to Jesus. Workmanship means masterpiece. God said I knew you before I formed you in your mother's womb. He is the potter. We are the clay. God knows what He is doing. We belong to God. Some people have let people tell them who they are. Ask God, "What is my purpose?" God's Got A Plan beyond the mess I'm in. When I have a purpose I cannot do what everybody else is doing. That's like kicking against the pricks like Paul did when he was persecuting the Saints of Jesus Christ. Only what I do for Christ Jesus will last. NOW is not the time to question my faith. Now is not the time to throw in the towel.

Sep 1, 2017, 6:54 AM

When He Knows your Name

St. John 10:3 To him the porter openeth; and the sheep hear his voice: and he calleth his own sheep by name, and leadeth them out.

"What a precious thought! My Jesus knows me by my name. I'm not a number, not a symbol, not just one in a series. I belong to Him and He knows my name. What joy and what security! Indeed, this is my point of identity and the basis for my self-esteem. Ah, sweet fellowship for I am His and He is mine!

Blessed Shepherd, the comfort of knowing that you know

me by name is beyond all measure. When I feel insignificant and afraid, let me hear Your voice tenderly calling and find security in knowing that I am Yours and You are mine." - Ann Shorb

Dec 10, 2020, 6:42 AM

Happy Monday! It's Ok to be different. God is colorful and made us fearfully and wonderfully – ALL un-apologetically. We are ALL beautiful in His eyes - like beautiful flowers. You are not a mistake. You were made on purpose.

Dec 2, 2013, 6:00 AM

I refuse to insult God by saying "I am a Defeated child of GOD Almighty"

"NO!!!!! Despite ALL these things, overwhelming victory is OURS THROUGH Christ, who loved us." Rom. 8:37 [NLT]

Dec 20, 2013, 4:44 PM

I looked to people for my identity. Now I look to God's Word for my identity.

Jun 13, 2013, 6:23 PM

I was made on purpose. I love the me who God made me to be.

Jul 4, 2013, 1:15 AM

Hey you! Yeah YOU. You are Christ Jesus' treasure. He loves YOU with an EVERLASTING Love...yeah YOU...and beyond what you could have EVER imagined - millions of eons from now HE will STILL Love you. I KNOW my husband probably couldn't Love ME that long but Jesus can. Hallelujah!

Aug 1, 2013, 12:11 AM

I am the Body of Christ. My body is the house of God. God lives in me and I belong to Him. I've been bought with the price of the blood of Jesus, so I glorify God in my body and in my spirit – 1 Corinthians 6:15-19; 2 Corinthians 6:16, 3:16. Give no place to the devil.

Nov 14, 2013, 12:00 AM

CHAPTER 7

God, the Waymaker

The asteroid won't hit earth because GOD told it not to hit earth. He told it to pass by earth and DON'T TOUCH IT. What a mighty God we serve. I BELIEVE and TRUST IN GOD more than ANY astronomer. I feel calm. There is no anxiety here because I feel the Grace of God.

Mar 6, 2014, 7:07 AM

Dawn Kellum was watching Dawn's Unseen Journey.

I am thankful for a heart of faith and I may not see my whole way clear; but I'm going to trust that GOD will make a way. If He did it before, He will do it again. What He's done for others, HE WILL do for me. The same God back then is the same God right now. Hebrews 13:8 Jesus Christ the same yesterday, and to day, and for ever.

Nov 17, 2014, 6:44 AM

Your Father in Heaven, the God of Abraham, Isaac and Jacob, will sustain you if you could just simply trust Him. If He feeds the birds, He will surely take care of you.

Things were tough financially for my family and I near the

end of 2019 as my husband was laid off due to the GM strike for over a month. I was working for the schools part-time as a substitute lunch aide and working to build my consulting business investing an average of $30 a month into the business to keep it up. I was still paying tithes and offering exercising my faith in God. Somehow, the Lord made a way for us.

A company paid hundreds of dollars to keep our lights on. Our rent got paid through a compassionate source. Strangers dropped off a load of healthy food from Costco the night before our food stamps were shutoff unexpectedly. On Thanksgiving and Christmas, we shared tables with our parents on both sides. Our 2005 car held out. We went to a junkyard out in the country and got a $60 part for $10 from a similar vehicle. A company gave us food for our Thanksgiving meal. Out of nowhere, a law firm contacted us in December and told us we had a nearly $1000 refund coming back from the sale of our home in 2016. The check has been successfully processed. I was hired as a hospice music therapist AND offered a long-term part time lunch aide position with a local Montessori academy. My youngest daughter got accepted to a local private Christian school. My son was offered multiple jobs after interviewing.

Sometime before Christmas 2019, my Heavenly Father gave me a vision of a lot of people giving me 250 of something. I didn't know what it was but I kept expecting it. Well, the entire unsolicited gift cards my family and I received over Christmastime from random strangers and some friends totaled $250. Another close friend gave me an additional $200.

Boast in the Lord's goodness. The Lord set it on my heart to share this and I hope you are inspired.

Jan 15, 2020, 6:28 AM

I am claiming a Divine and Supernatural breakthrough in EVERY aspect of my life, i.e., spiritually, mentally, emotionally, financially, etc.

My pastor said Sunday to ask God, "HELP MY UNBELIEF." God has shown MIRACULOUS things and my FAITH is INCREASING to outstanding levels.

I have already witnessed MANY miracles this week; a Miraculous Healing, things broke that were fixed, food and money multiplying, emotional and spiritual breakthroughs and more.

Jesus is a miracle worker.

Apr 2, 2014, 2:36 PM

God will provide. Yesterday, I paid tithes on what I made in addition to what I WANTED to make on my second job and right after paying them the sales came flowing in like never before! Trust God. Won't He do it!

Oct 20, 2014, 6:47 AM

Dawn Kellum was watching Jesus work.

Friday, November 28, 2014, the Holy Spirit told me to hold my 4-year-old's hand tight as we exited the subway onto the platform at 59th street/3rd avenue in NYC. I am glad I listened because my daughter's foot slipped between the train and the platform and, thankfully, I was able to pull her up because I held her hand tight; otherwise, her leg would have gotten caught between the train and the platform! I said, "Thank you Jesus!"

THEN she started crying and said her shoe came off! Her shoe had fallen onto the subway tracks! Once the train left, I thought, "Oh well. We will have to buy her some new shoes." THEN suddenly my husband jumped down onto the subway tracks to get his baby's shoe! People were telling him "NO. DON'T DO IT!" I told him, "NO!" I was in complete shock! I called on JESUS! My husband was able to grab her shoe, throw it back on the platform, and quickly jump over a 6 foot high wall after 2 failed attempts! 15 SECONDS later another subway train came! He could have gotten killed! I said, "Thank you Jesus!" I had to sit down for a few minutes to gain my composure! I told my husband he didn't have to do that and that we could have bought her some more shoes. His answer was, "I'm NOT gonna' let my baby walk around in the cold with only one shoe on!" I am STILL in SHOCK and thankful for divine protection!

Dec 1, 2014, 5:12 AM

Dawn Kellum is feeling blessed.

I prayed & asked God for a financial breakthrough. I did NOT expect what I received today. We attained over $15,000 in addition to our current income to help with living expenses for the entire year, a raise and a new comfortable Kingsize Bed after sleeping on blow-up beds for months! Seek ye FIRST the kingdom of God, and his righteousness; and all these things shall be added unto you. Matthew 6:33 (KJV) Take care of God's house and I am a Witness GOD WILL TAKE GOOD CARE OF YOUR HOUSE!

Jan 12, 2015, 10:11 PM

...sending prayers out for all of us, including myself, affected by this General Motors layoff. Know that God is the source of all of our needs and, as we trust Him, He will sustain us. God Bless and much.

Apr 25, 2016, 6:35 AM

July 2016, my beloved brother-in-law passed away. He was a hard-working Father of 12 children and well-loved by many. My 2 young daughters and I headed to Georgia from Michigan to be with my grieving Sister and family.

I had no other driver to assist me driving because my husband had to work. I reached out to my church family to ask for prayer.

Well, I drove through the night. I left town about 5PM. I took 2 caffeine pills to help stay woke (later in the year I suffered a heart attack due to me developing caffeine sensitivity – so please don't take caffeine pills).

My van was in bad shape. The muffler was being held up by a wire hanger; my turn signals weren't working all too great and my windshield wipers often clashed due to a windshield wiper synchronization problem that no shop seemed able to fix. There was little traffic so the drive was not too bad until it started raining vehemently. I put on my windshield wipers and they would clash almost consistently. I could barely see the road. Suddenly, lightning flashed across the sky to light up the road where the light was needed. This happened multiple times during the 13 hour trip. God is concerned about your situation. He hears. He sees. He knows. He doesn't skip a beat. Thank God for allowing the lightning to light up the road to help lead the way. There were other miraculous occurrences also on the way. God's presence is amazing.

With men this was impossible; but with God all things were possible.

Sep 16, 2015, 4:59 AM

Dawn Kellum updated her status.

"Have no fear. God is with you." That is what God gave me as I traveled almost 100 miles in heavy flood waters, heavy rain & near-zero visibility last night. The lightning LIT the freeway when I couldn't see the road. Thank you God.

Jun 8, 2015, 6:58 AM

Life has MANY storms; however, look at the one who has ALL POWER OVER THE STORMS in His Hands. Know also that Jesus Christ can see the end and the beginning of all storms. Trust Him.

There is no storm in the believer's life that He is not aware of. Know that He is with you always even unto the end of the age and that you have the victory through Him. You are an overcomer through Christ Jesus. Trust Him. Never doubt. Believe Him.

Jun 25, 2015, 10:01 PM

Dawn Kellum updated her status.

Look for the escape route through your temptation. There hath no temptation taken you but such as is common to man: but God is faithful, who will not suffer YOU to be tempted above that ye are able; but will WITH the temptation also make a way to escape, that ye may be able to bear it.

Jan 8, 2016, 5:23 AM

Dawn Kellum updated her status.

....just closed on the sale of our home free and clear. The house was sold the first day on the market. Won't God do it!!!

Jan 14, 2016, 10:38 AM

Dawn Kellum updated her status.

...just got a call. I got the job. I start the day that I trusted GOD's plan to start and not my plan. Trust God's timing. Amen.

Jan 13, 2016, 8:28 AM

My daughter got the Holy Ghost today! I'm SO grateful. Thank you Jesus! Hallelujah! I cried so hard with tears of joy and she was so happy!

Mar 13, 2016, 4:31 PM

What is the message in this situation? My 5 yr old locked the children's bathroom door and closed it??! I spent hours trying multiple methods, doing research and more, but I couldn't open that door. God spoke and said, "Ask me." I said, "God I know that you're able to open this door." He said, "...knowing that I can do something is not asking. Ask me." I then asked Him to open the door; believing He could. Within a matter of seconds the door popped open! I immediately got chills ALL over!!!??

Apr 10, 2016, 7:36 AM

Angels at the science festival: My family and I went to a very crowded science festival yesterday at MSU's Biomedical and Physical Sciences building. My daughter was at an exhibit where she had to shoot a small brick with a slingshot within a large cardboard box. My daughter is very strong and shot the brick at an angle OUT the box and about 40 feet PAST the box! I prayed immediately and saw this same brick bypass a bunch of people in a very crowded room and fly through a very small space between people hitting NOONE and then the floor. Thank you Jesus for protecting those people and answering my prayer! Hallelujah!!

Apr 8, 2018, 7:50 AM

I am grateful for the $7.03 check I received yesterday from a settlement from years ago. Count your blessings. Name them one by one.

Jul 27, 2016, 9:14 PM

I came home from the Called Women's conference held at BreadHouse yesterday and had 3 miracles in my mailbox!! I also gained additional prophetic insight on how to pray for every woman, lady and girl in my life as well as how to be a better wife and so much more.

Nov 13, 2016, 6:11 AM

I just had a flat on the freeway in the middle of rush hour traffic going in excess of 70 miles per hour. I rode the merge medians AND the side of the freeway for miles on a flat to get off the freeway. I barely hit guard rails, cars and trucks speeding; but I'm grateful I made it off the freeway. Thank God for His grace!!

Nov 22, 2016, 7:57 AM

I just got a free cart of groceries from Walmart right after I blessed my family with $$ to buy dinner for themselves. Give and it shall be given unto you.

Mar 12, 2017, 3:31 PM

I just received a $65.00 energy bill in February! Can't nobody do me like Jesus. God will make a way.

Mar 15, 2017, 7:10 AM

Testimony: My tire rim was broke. Mechanic was surprised that the tire hadn't popped yet. Many places quoted us nearly $200 for a rim. Many junkyards didn't have it. I then prayed today for God to show us where to go. We drove approx. 12 miles to a junkyard in the country and walked through a huge muddy junkyard. They had our SAME vehicle! We got a good steel - not aluminum - rim WITH a tire for $20!!! Now I'm trusting God for these car turn signals & headlights.

Moral-Cant nobody do me like Jesus. Acknowledge the Lord in all your ways and He will direct your paths. GOD is the source for all our needs. Go straight to the source.

Apr 8, 2017, 1:13 PM

Dawn Kellum updated her status.

How did a $958 estimated engine job turn into an actual $120 engine job? The answer is favor. I'm grateful and thankful.

Sep 9, 2017, 5:34 PM

...that moment you take advice from Heaven through your Pastor's Sunday message and "Stand Still" and then get promoted within 90 days of starting a new job while people around you lookin' at you crazy.

May 23, 2017, 12:37 PM

Pray continually. Never give up. Stand on God's word. He cannot lie. God will provide. As a child of God you are precious to him. Know that He hears your cry like a parent hears the cries of their beloved child. Trust God and His plans. I've been praying for you; for the homeless in the streets and the ones on drugs; the mothers raising children on their own. Jesus Christ loves you

Jesus Christ is praying that your faith fail not. Be delivered from drugs in the name of Jesus Christ. Don't lose heart. God is able to provide you shelter and everything you need. My family and I were homeless, but God blessed us with a home. My husband and I were unemployed and God blessed us with jobs. God is sending help your way for you and your family.

Trust God. Believe. Have faith. Keep hope alive. Love one another. Show love to one another and pray.

Guide me Great Jehovah. Holy Spirit lead.

Oct 8, 2017, 8:48 AM

Bishop Nemiah Smith is never forgotten! When I came back to the Lord many years ago about 7 months pregnant and very weak spiritually, this man of God helped me and my boyfriend - now husband - Nolan get back in fellowship with God. He also gave us pre-marital and marital counseling, was a great spiritual father and so much more. He also signed our Marriage license. We are still holding on to God and to each other going on over 20 years and never separated. My husband was delivered of alcohol addiction through the ministry of Jesus Christ at Greater Apostolic Faith under the pastoral leadership of Bishop Nemiah Smith. I thank God for God's children being in me and my family's lives.

Feb 23, 2018, 7:13 AM

...when you leave work rushing to find a store still open that sells a special chemical flask for your 5th grader's science project AND, once you find a store that may or may not have one, your sweet sister in Christ is already there and knows exactly where one is. It was $2.99!!

May 16, 2018, 6:49 AM

..miracles happening left and right! I've got a seed in the ground. Everything is working together for the good. One planted and another watered but GOD gives the increase.

May 16, 2018, 7:00 AM

The preacher preached, "I want what belongs to me." I place the soles of my feet on whatever belongs to me and I'll go wherever He leads because I know it's time to reap. God promised Abraham that He would bless those who bless him. Look beyond the roughness of this life. Trust God to the core that He will work it out His way. Get your mind off things that are not for you. Don't be so focused on going after something that doesn't belong to you so that you become paralyzed.

God has already bound the strong man and prepared a way for you to handle the tough situation in front of you. Consider Joshua and Caleb who spied out the land in Numbers Chapter 13 and said that we are more than able to conquer them. How dare we come into God's presence arrogantly as if we can't Praise Him. Praise Him like you know He has it all worked out. Thank God for the mountains because, as long as Jesus is your friend, you have the victory.

Deuteronomy chapter 8 verse 3 God suffered thee to hunger and fed thee with manna or angels' food. It's hard looking at a situation that is tough when you consider your own strength but with God all things are possible. If it is God's will, God has already gone before you to prepare your victory. Serve God like you're a winner. Say, "I can do all things through Christ Jesus who strengthens me. Greater is He that is in me than he that is in the world."

Deuteronomy 9: 1 - 2 Deuteronomy 8:2 - 3 Deuteronomy 11:24 Philippians 4:13 Joshua 1:3 - 4

Nov 13, 2017, 7:46 AM

The Lord has blessed my Dad so much since he was dire sick in the hospital a little while ago. He was singing, dancing and playing his bass guitar at Sunday night Joy night service this week as I lead the testimonial service. Can't nobody do us like Jesus!!

Jun 2, 2018, 6:53 AM

My baby got the Holy Ghost today!!

Sep 30, 2018, 4:48 PM

"What happens when the brook dries up? God is preparing a blessing to come your way. Hold on. Help is on the way. Reinforcements are on the way. Strength is on the way. Joy and peace is on the way. The angel got a blessing in his hand." - Bishop LW Gates

He is coming to your home, your job or your situation. Hold on. Somebody say glory. Weeping may endure for a night but joy is coming in the morning. Hold on. Trust God. Keep hope alive. I dance and jump because I am grateful. God has turned my mourning into dancing my ashes into beauty. Some would say I've lost it but I have found my joy.

Dec 28, 2018, 7:29 AM

......within the last 2 days I received a miraculous healing testimony and a separate approximate $1000 financial break-through. I have many more testimonies too. Only God has done these things. Trust God. Serve in the kingdom.

Feb 20, 2019, 6:26 PM

There is nobody like our God.....when God heals you miraculously from an illness you suffered with for nearly 34 years AND your dentist does root canal therapy (approx. $1000 -$2000) for free AND your income taxes come back in less than 2 weeks with an increased adjustment AND you get divine favor on your job AND you are chosen as one of ten finalists for a big gospel singing competition ALL WITHIN ONE MONTH!

Mar 9, 2019, 8:41 AM

Thank you Jesus for giving me the strength to finish my 3rd 13.1 mile/half-marathon race today in approximately 3 hours and roughly 10 minutes. Approximately 15 years ago I was diagnosed with heart failure, fainting sporadically and prescribed atenolol! My Dad prayed for me and told me not to take the medicine. I believed God for my healing and signed up for my 1st half-marathon. I was determined to launch out on faith. I eventually recovered!!

During the race today there was a lot of heavy, cold wind resistance and very steep hills, but I made it! I also managed to find the strength to take my loving Sister-in-Law out for her birthday today. Happy Birthday Sheresa!

Apr 13, 2019, 5:58 PM

..reflecting on a sermon from 3/31/19

"It's not what it looks like." We got a notice that rent would increase by $140 a month when we renew the lease?! A sermon was preached Sunday 3/31/19 of the same week. I followed instructions from the sermon. Today, I received a call from the Landlord stating that rent would ONLY increase by $20. Thank you Jesus for making a way for me and my family.

Apr 9, 2019, 6:30 PM

...this came in the mail yesterday. All of our cars are PAID OFF IN FULL. THANK YOU JESUS!

Apr 11, 2019, 7:49 AM

God will protect and provide. We sold one of our cars on Facebook Marketplace this week within 24 hours of its posting for the amount we asked God for. The buyer, a complete stranger, offered to pick up the car the same day by 8:20 PM (very dark at that time) in the evening at our apartment complex. While we waited, I prayed and asked my heavenly Father to protect us. The buyer showed up about 8:05 PM with a flatbed connected to a big black truck with black tinted windows on the 2nd row.

During our transaction, I then started to see all kinds of people come out; a Man with a little boy walking, a couple drove up that started talking outside, another man out in the dark walking his dog, another car which drove up right next to us and another two people walked at a short distance. After the transaction, we looked to Heaven and said, "Thank you Jesus." God will provide and protect you!

Sep 30, 2019, 8:59 AM

Wisdom Wednesday: Family, since I quit my job in May 2019 because I refused to compromise my faith AND due to us having to urgently remove our daughter from her elementary school, God has taught my husband and I a lot.

-Trust God even when facing compromise. God will take care of you.

-God is in control so He doesn't need our help - just follow Him.

-Appreciate everything God gives.

-Worship Him even through the process. He will give you much wisdom in your spirit during this time.

-Acknowledge Him in all your ways so He can direct your paths. "Father, please show me...."

-Don't take the counsel of the ungodly, but take pleasure in the laws of God.

-We have seen firsthand the suffering and trials of the most vulnerable in our society. Be more compassionate to people. See where the real needs are. Many are forced to make harsh decisions just to take care of their families.

-The world hated Jesus first and, being in Him, you will also be hated by those who love the world more than God. The eternal rewards are out of this world though. That is speaking literally!

-God has exposed Christians who are more focused on

trying to protect their pocketbooks than standing for true Christ-righteousness.

-You will feel hate but remain LOVE because you abide in Jesus

-As a child of God, nothing happens to you unless He allows it for a reason. LISTEN to what God is saying in whatever situation. Worship Him to hear Him better.

-The devil has no power over you and sin will never take control if you abide in Jesus. Love Him more.

-God has set our natural house into His divine order and blessed our family abundantly.

-God is blessing our family business. A grant is being received for our new office area about 5 miles from our home.

- God has opened doors and given much wisdom in multiple areas in our lives.

- God loves you more than anybody ever could or would.

- God will never leave you nor forsake you.

- We are encouraged and holding onto our faith in God through it all. We will continue to run on, as God gives us grace, to see what the end will be.

Jul 24, 2019, 10:48 AM

Thankful Thursdays - Be Encouraged. God knows what you and your family needs. He has already figured out how He will provide. I can feel portions of the impenetrable walls turning into doors being opened by God, and we receive all God has for us.

Oct 3, 2019, 7:42 AM

The Lord is my light. I've seen God move the mountains and I believe I'll see Him do it again, but if He doesn't move the mountains, I still know that He is able. God's ways are higher and better than our ways. Trust God's plan. God holds our future in His hands.

Faith over fear. Do God's will and seek His purpose for your life. The battle belongs to the Lord. Use His weapons to fight spiritual battles. Jesus won, is winning and will always win.

Matt 6:9; Psalms 23; II Chron 7:13-14; Psalm 91; Heb 11:6

Mar 13, 2020, 6:23 AM

Be encouraged even if you can't see the light at the end of the tunnel. There is a hill or bridge coming, and at the end, you will see the light. In the meantime trust the conductor.

Dec 21, 2019, 9:11 AM

God will MAKE a way. Keep trusting and believing Him.

Dec 16, 2019, 6:25 PM

I am grateful for our Christmas miracle. Whenever we fall short, our heavenly Father handles the rest.

Dec 19, 2019, 6:44 AM

When God speaks!!! When we sold our house in 2015, a gentleman in county government was trying to hold up the sale of our house by consistently telling us we had to pay for all kinds of warranties, add-ons, etc. before we went to closing.

He was also in cohorts with the person responsible for managing our septic tank – so he too was telling us that a 3- 5 year warranty had to be purchased before we went to closing. We were running out of funds. We continued to pray to Jesus by the leading of the Holy Spirit.

We still sold our house the first day on the market (my sister and my cousin cleaned/prepared the house immaculately). We sold it "As Is" for CASH and for approx. $12000 more than what we purchased it for approx. 3 years prior. Also a cousin of mine and a sister-in-law touched and agreed with me in 2011 that I would sell the house in 3 years!

I went up to the county government office to inquire further about what was needed in order to go to closing. A lady in county government wrote a letter giving us authorization to go to closing!! She said, "I don't know why that gentleman [who had a high role] was sending you those emails telling you those things were required! He is on vacation! I sent the letter out to you and you can now go to closing."

It doesn't matter what evil comes your way to stop God's plans. If God wants something to happen. It WILL happen. Stay faithful to God. Know and learn His voice and take action when He tells you. Boast in God's goodness. He is true and faithful to every promise He makes. God will take care of you.

Jan 5, 2020, 9:11 AM

God didn't bring us this far to leave us with no hope or direction. Trust Him. Are You Listening?

Feb 11, 2020, 9:59 PM

Testimony: My nieces had an amazing idea to incorporate a virtual learning experience into their Friday evening youth bible quiz and project virtual participants to a screen so those physically present may see and hear them. God gave the wisdom and allowed me to purchase an indoor/outdoor theater kit ($2000 projector and a $400 laptop) for a total of $200!!!

Later on that evening I had a vision of my sister who recently passed away walking back and forth rejoicing about God making a way! Wow! I can't explain how God does and/or allows things, but I love having a relationship with my heavenly Father. Praise God!

Jul 4, 2020, 7:20 AM

A couple days ago my daughter and I were aggressively encountered by my new neighbor's loose dog on our way to our apartment door. The dog was masterfully beautiful, big and black like midnight. This dog was not trying to listen to its owner, but found it necessary to try to attack us. As I consistently knocked on the door patiently waiting on my husband to open the door, I knew I had to stand my ground and fight it if necessary. I love dogs, but if they attack me or my kids, I may have to intercede aggressively.

My young daughter with me quickly retreated to somewhere in another hallway. The dog tried to go after her but I commanded, "Get Back. Get over here!" As I continued to intently look the dog in the eye with the authority of God backing me, I loudly commanded multiple times, "Get Back! Get over there! No! You do not! You go over there!" I never turned my back on the dog and, while still giving commands, I started to see fear in the dog's eyes. Eventually it retreated back to its owner. The dog's owner watched in horror and was looking at me in awe. I had a few "Motherly Words of Wisdom" for the owner too.

Word from Heaven. Resist the devil with the word and power of God and he will flee! Live the kind of life where the enemy sees God in you and knows who you belong to. You must know WHO you are and WHOSE you are. You are safe in Jesus even when your loved ones turn their back on you, run out of fear or take a long time coming to your rescue because they don't recognize the SERIOUSNESS of what you're going through.

Jul 8, 2020, 7:58 AM

...after service yesterday, hubby and I went to go speak and minister a word from God to one of my friends, who just happens to be a local multi-millionaire. We were ABUN-DANTLY blessed in the process and he didn't want us to leave. God's favor is real. It's okay to love people for real - like for real.

Jul 20, 2020, 8:21 AM

I'm thankful for my family's new much needed ride and my new work from home job with a wonderful company so I can be at home with my babies while they attend school virtu-ally. I am also very thankful for having the presence and peace of God in my household in the midst of a pandemic and even after suffering the loss of my Dad, my big Sister, my Aunt, my cousins and other beloved loved ones all within a matter of months. God is a mind regulator and a heart fixer.

Aug 8, 2020, 9:43 AM

Dawn Kellum updated her status.

Wow. I paid $3 for hundreds of dollars worth of dental work and got an unexpected check in the mail for $$$ from an unexpected premium rebate from nearly a year ago. This all just happened today!!

Sep 28, 2020, 5:06 PM

There were completely unexpected monies in my account today in the hundreds. Wow! The more I give to help others, the more I receive.

Sep 14, 2020, 4:36 PM

God will take care of you. I just got over $200 worth of brand new clothes for less than $13 at an unexpected 1-day sale.

Dec 5, 2020, 2:29 PM

I can do all things through Christ Jesus who continues to strengthen me. It doesn't matter how slow or how fast the race is run. Finish the race and do it well. I believed God to take me to the finish line of a 13.1 mile half-marathon!! I believed God to give me the strength to make it to the goal and I did! I had the heart of a finisher.

Have the heart of a finisher and never stop believing God until you get your miracle. Then believe that He will carry you further and give even more victories! Keep pressing and moving in faith. It's not time to give up trusting God for your miracle. God is STILL working miracles!! Sometimes when we believe God for miracles, we have to humble ourselves, pray, seek His face, repent and turn from our ungodly and unholy ways. I had to do this a few times. Thank you Jesus for grace!

Oct 19, 2020, 10:37 AM

Dawn Kellum is feeling grateful.

Good Morning. I woke up to a dead cell phone. I became so upset because I need my cell phone to login with 2-factor authentication in order to work. I found out the charger wasn't giving enough power to the cell phone in order for it to turn on. Thankfully, I was able to use another backup charger at home. The phone STILL wasn't coming on after waiting about 20 minutes for it to charge with the backup charger. Pressing the power button and removing the battery several times was not working!

Then a thought came, "Pray that Jesus restore the power to your cell phone like your friend Jeanita did before her power was restored after a power outage." I then touched the power button on the phone and said, "Jesus, please restore the power to my cell phone." IMMEDIATELY THE PHONE STARTED TO LOAD!!! Hallelujah!!!

Oct 23, 2020, 8:32 AM

When God Speaks: Last year, during a tough financial time for my family, the Lord spoke to me in a vision and showed me getting a SPECIFIC amount of something. I didn't know what it was, but it totaled a specific amount. Well, a few weeks later, MULTIPLE people gave my family and I what totaled that specific amount in gift cards - all unsolicited.

Fast forward to about a year later. A few days ago the Lord spoke to me in a vision and said the employer (either my job or my husband's job) would give us rent for one month AND another month. Well, my husband told me yesterday that his job is giving him a huge holiday stipend for this month of November and for December.

At last night's Called Women's Conference, Lady Singleton said, "When God promises, it will come to pass." Hallelujah

Nov 14, 2020, 5:18 AM

God will MAKE a way. God Has MADE a way. God IS MAKING a way. Praise GOD because He will MAKE a way, He has MADE a way and He is MAKING a way. Shout to GOD because He will MAKE a way, He has MADE a way and He is MAKING a way, etc. Hallelujah!

Sep 26, 2013, 10:07 PM

When you are truly thankful to God AND appreciate the friends, family, houses, stuff, etc. He has allowed you to have; He will continue to bless you beyond measure. I just got a

HUGE windfall of a LOT of stuff me and my babies needed AND more - Thank you God! JEHOVAH JIREH.

Sep 10, 2013, 8:39 PM

What just happened??? I prayed and asked God, "Lord please bless my husband with ANOTHER job in his field" A company just called a few minutes ago to ask me if I was available...and I said "My husband is. He is in the same field" HIS INTERVIEW IS TOMORROW!!!! (REJOICING)

Oct 31, 2013, 10:06 AM

To all of us (including me and my family) with NO electricity or heat in our houses - even if we feel like the power companies have forgotten about us, just remember that GOD is the source of ALL power and HAS NOT FORGOTTEN ABOUT US. Be Encouraged.

Dec 23, 2013, 6:47 PM

I thank God for my brother and my Sister-in-law opening up their home to my family and I until our power is restored from the Winter Storm Outage. The estimated restoration time is 12.28.13 @11:30PM. We have been here since Sunday. We are feeling loved and grateful.

Dec 23, 2013, 7:20 PM

My house still has no power (electricity or gas), but, during prayer this morning, God gave me this song.

"Great is Thy faithfulness!" "Great is Thy faithfulness!"

Morning by morning new mercies I see;

All I have needed Thy hand hath provided—

"Great is Thy faithfulness," Lord, unto me!
Dec 27, 2013, 1:18 PM

TESTIMONY: Take care of God's House. He will take care of yours. My Hubby and Son were shoveling snow at the church today. On the way home from church Hubby got STUCK coming up the driveway. A stranger QUICKLY came along with a snow-plow truck and offered to shovel the ENTIRE DRIVEWAY!??!? It was a 5-car semi-circular driveway with almost 2 FEET of snow! Amazing!
Jan 5, 2014, 5:19 PM

TESTIMONY: I prayed a Gideon prayer 3 years ago and said "Jesus, if it is your will for me to remain in Lansing for a time, please bless me with THIS specific job".

I got my desired position a few days later. The manager said that he was trying to get in contact with me after waiting some time for a response. This week marks 3 years at this same job. I am a witness that if your initial desire is to serve God more, He will GIVE you the desires of your heart. One "YES" from God outweighs ANY "No" so Be Encouraged, if He wants you to have it, YOU WILL!!
Jan 11, 2014, 7:38 PM

TESTIMONY (TEARS): I went to church today and gave a SACRIFICIAL offering - like the widow's offering (Ref. Luke 21:1-4) and said, "God, you hold tomorrow and will provide for my needs anyway - so I will still give to your kingdom out of my very LITTLE because I ALREADY Know you WILL Provide for my needs."

Once I got home, an individual I haven't seen in a LONG time POPPED UP at my house OUT OF THE BLUE from a long way across town to say, "Somebody blessed me with this $$$$; but, God said it wasn't for me. God told me that it was for YOU!!??"

Jan 12, 2014, 3:20 PM

Dawn Kellum was watching God Work It Out.

TESTIMONY: I went to a tire shop to find out what was wrong with my tires. During the wait, I said "Jesus. Lord. Please bless ME however." They said one tire had TREAD SEPARATION and showed it to me. It could have caused a MAJOR accident!!!?? They told me I needed to pay about $100 to get a new tire. I asked them to use the spare underneath the van INSTEAD!

Fast Forward - Amazingly, they were NOT able to bring the spare from the bottom of the van SO THEY GAVE ME A FREE TIRE and told me to NOT PAY ANYTHING. God WILL provide!

Jan 17, 2014, 8:45 PM

CHAPTER 8

Matters of Money

Dawn Kellum updated her status.

Question: Investing in an eternal Kingdom's treasures VS investing in a temporary Kingdom's treasures. If the eternal kingdom is the entire pie and the temporary kingdom is 0.00000000000000000001% of that pie which calculates to LESS THAN NOTHING, which yields the most value?

Feb 25, 2015, 6:43 AM

Matthew 19:24 Again I tell you, it is easier for a camel to go through the eye of a needle than for a rich person to enter the kingdom of God."

Apr 19, 2014, 11:28 AM

What we TRULY value is evidenced in our checkbooks and calendars. Now, what does JESUS CHRIST value??

Jun 12, 2014, 8:20 PM

Dawn Kellum is feeling peaceful.

Drastic times require drastic measures. The more materialistic things we have - the more problems we acquire. Too many people spend too much time stressing over what is really the small STUFF. Too many people spend too much time AND money trying to hold on to STUFF. It's time to give up some STUFF to have some peace.

Sep 2, 2014, 1:09 PM

God is the source of my supply. My employment is only a REsource and not THE Source. Trust in God and NOT your REsource. Resources are not solid foundations but God is. Oh yes! God is.

Jun 4, 2015, 6:59 AM

"Money is numbers and numbers never end. If it takes money to be happy, your search for happiness will never end." - Bob Marley

Oct 16, 2017, 10:07 PM

If anyone doesn't take care of his own relatives, especially his immediate family, he has denied the Christian faith and is worse than an unbeliever. I Timothy 5:8 GOD'S WORD Translation

Oct 1, 2017, 7:58 AM

Word of Wisdom to those with car notes: Avoid car repossession. Call your car loan company and request to pay ONLY interest until you can afford to pay the entire car note again. YES. It exists.

Nov 19, 2015, 12:53 PM

Sometimes those of us who are Christians with a lot of

money and huge networks invest in what we or others see as the "big-league" stuff to fulfill our goals and passions God has given us. Here is the kicker though. Sometimes those God-given desires and passions require that our excess money and huge networks be removed so we will see the power of Jehovah Jireh fulfill those desires and passions miraculously on our behalf. Praise Him through it even if it doesn't make sense. Look to Him for direction. Let our God of wonders beyond this galaxy arise as the one who has all power in His hands. Remember Him as the God who can turn kings' hearts as the rivers of waters. God will make or create a way as He does all the time. Let God work. Rejoice in your inabilities to do what YOU see as the best way and surrender to Him as the one who is stronger in our weakness. In my life be glorified Oh God. Why put trust in people who are fickle anyway? Trust God.

Aug 1, 2019, 2:02 PM

Father, I hear you. Speak Lord.

Hebrews 13:5 ESV Keep your life free from love of money, and be content with what you have, for he has said, "I will never leave you nor forsake you."

Matthew 16:26 ESV What shall a man give in return for his soul?

1 Timothy 6:9-10 ESV. But those who desire to be rich fall into temptation, into a snare, into many senseless and harmful desires that plunge people into ruin and destruction. For the love of money is a root of all kinds of evils. It is through this craving that some have wandered away from the faith and pierced themselves with many pangs.

Jul 12, 2019, 6:50 PM

Riddle: The ***** in your life can become your god when you don't have it AND/OR when you have it. When you don't have what you *****, you spend countless hours trying to get that *****. When you do have what you *****, you spend countless hours trying to prevent from losing it. Your ***** is where your heart is. Don't be deceived.

Jul 23, 2019, 7:50 PM

God wants us - not our money, although I faithfully tithe, give freely and support the kingdom of Jesus Christ on this earth. The church needs the money to continue the ministry of Jesus Christ on this earth. God wants our whole heart. Why don't we just want God or to commune with God? Why do we JUST want His riches? When we get to that forever-living place in eternity, will we just want to bask in the riches and richness of that place or, more importantly, commune with God in His presence? Would you rather live to be in His presence or just let your belly be your god? When you have God, you have everything. I shall be satisfied in my heavenly Father's will. I also have learned that everything I need is in Him, and that He also gives the desires of your heart. Ultimately, I found that His presence is so much more valuable than anything - no matter where I am.

Oct 6, 2019, 10:12 AM

Some of us obey our pocketbooks more than our Heavenly Father. Father, please help us to do your will.

Sep 25, 2019, 8:35 PM

The salary that sin pays is eternal death. We were talking to one of our multi-millionaire associates yesterday evening. They brought up a discussion to encourage us to do something deceitful for increased material objects. I immediately interjected and said "No. We will look up to God and ask Him to make it right so we don't have to lie. That's what we do." The individual responded in a Matthew 4 "tone" and started mentioning how things could be a whole lot better for us. If you have to sin to get it or keep it, then it's not from Jesus Christ and it will cause you great grief. WWJD (What would Jesus do?)

Sep 26, 2019, 9:45 AM

When I had a 6-figure income, I chose to invest money into tithing and offering and giving to various holistic (healthy mind, body and spirit) ministries, my household and individuals in need. When I no longer had anywhere near a 6 figure income, Yeshua (Jesus Christ) sustained me and my household.

Mar 12, 2020, 7:03 AM

Don't be the one with a poverty mindset stealing from your own self, your own dreams and the poor you could be helping.

Feb 20, 2020, 8:48 PM

If we LOVE money, fame or fortune, we may wander away from the faith and have much grief. LOVE God. Be a seeker of God. In Pursuit Of God 2020 And Beyond is my goal.

Feb 17, 2020, 7:47 AM

..just went to the grocery store and saw a wad of cash on the floor. I immediately started asking people around me if it was theirs. Nobody claimed it. I tried to get the attention of a store associate, but they completely ignored me multiple times and kept walking. I then audibly told the people around me, "Well. It's not mine." I then proceeded to walk away. Thou shalt not steal. Amen.

Oct 26, 2020, 2:02 PM

Good Morning Everyone. I just said this to my pile of BILLS and Trying to Eliminate ALL Past due Bills. "Listen to me. I'm talking to you. Jesus Christ said you would obey me. In the name of the Lord Jesus Christ, I command you, I say to you, BE PAID IN FULL...DEMATERIALIZE...DEPART...BE GONE...IN JESUS CHRIST NAME, YOU WILL OBEY ME!"

Jun 3, 2013, 10:06 AM

Good Morning. Jehovah Jireh. What a miracle! I gotta' TESTIFY. This is the first time in almost 12 years that Hubby and I received ALL of our income tax back AND more. It was normally offset because of a huge past debt. I prayed a Gideon prayer to Jesus Christ and prayed a debt-elimination prayer from womenunspotted.com. Although the debt is still there, our income tax was not offset and Jesus Christ confirmed that the remaining debt would be paid off by the end of the year.

Jun 20, 2013, 7:37 AM

...gotta' share this testimony too. I also prayed a prayer for income-increase from womenunspotted.com and I have already made $10,000 - $15,000 MORE THAN this time last year at the same job. Praise God!

Jun 20, 2013, 7:42 AM

CHAPTER 9

Career Matters

Don't let the devil deceive you into being ungrateful for the blessings God has allowed you to have; otherwise, you will waste time, energy and resources seeking brown pastures which only appear to be green. Put that same time, energy and resources into what God has already blessed you with. I would like no distractions please.

Mar 19, 2015, 6:38 AM

Lesson: There will always be negatives in your professional life. If you focus on the negative instead of the positive, you'll miss out on great opportunities.

May 2, 2014, 6:19 PM

I KNOW that God has, is and will ALWAYS PROVIDE. My boss asked me to come in for a review. My review was considered HIGH PERFORMING, including, but not limited to maintaining honesty, integrity and MUCH MORE. He told me that I was being promoted to a Senior-Level Engineer Position WITH a pay increase $$$....

I did NOT ask to be promoted to that position. My boss

just placed me in it based off of my review. THAT WAS GOD. God IS concerned about our personal situations. Seek ye first the kingdom of God and HIS righteousness and everything pertaining to life and godliness will be added unto you. God Will Provide.

Aug 1, 2014, 7:02 PM

I received a "No" this week about a job I prayed & fasted earnestly to God for. It would have been a MUCH higher promotion than the one I just received. I was ready to give up and put in a 2-week notice; however, I kept praying & confessing the word of God from scriptures like Jeremiah 29:11, Phil 4;13, Psalms 121:1 and many more. I was waiting to hear from God FIRST before I made such a drastic move.

God kept telling me in my spirit, "Don't Give Up." I did NOT want to hear that- so I prayed again and thought, "maybe that wasn't God's voice." ALL types of NEGATIVE thoughts kept surfacing because I refused to take heed to God's VOICE. I prayed AGAIN and God said again, "Don't give up. I am still working on your behalf. I know your desires. I love you the most and want the best for you. THIS is a testing period where satan wants you to give up. Don't give up."

Then the Lord laid it on my heart to contact my friend and tell her my bad news. Her immediate response was brief and included the words, "DON'T GIVE UP!" Ha!

Sep 18, 2014, 10:28 PM

..when you're approved and given nearly $7000 to take the highest global defense course and certification given by the most respected defense training institute AND it can be taken

virtually. Then the company turned around and approved me for a huge raise. I am so humbled. GOD keeps on blessing me.
Mar 6, 2018, 6:53 AM

I had the chance to showcase my website www.womenunspotted.com and now my site, which spreads the gospel of Jesus Christ, is being viewed in countries around the world!
Sep 12, 2015, 7:27 AM

I am thankful for the 8 likes and ALL those who provide words of encouragement, prayers and so much more to my music ministry for our Lord. I appreciate the support and encouragement. Thank you SO much!! Hugs!
Apr 15, 2016, 5:18 AM

My venture recently got approved partnership with three billion-dollar cyber security firms and God sent me biz coaches making excess of millions per year who are very successful and so much more. Now it's time to work this.
Aug 18, 2016, 7:28 AM

...asked God 2 send me help 4 this new venture & He is doing that & so much more from unexpected sources. I am GRATEFUL. If you want your seed 2 grow, invest in it, nourish it, get help with it, feed it, etc.
Aug 15, 2016, 9:13 AM

NOTE: All of our skills and special talents that we use in our businesses, on the job, in our homes, etc. are all given to us by GOD (this does not include lying, stealing, cheating folks, etc.) GOD gives us the ability to make money and cut deals. He did it for our parents and mentors and he does it for us too. Be Encouraged.

Jul 27, 2016, 9:38 AM

You don't have to sin, use sex appeal or use your body as a weapon to be successful in the workplace. Just be honest, do good work, & seek to please God in all you do. Remember that God is the source of your blessings NOT that job or the people you work with.

Apr 6, 2017, 7:03 AM

A well-known billion- dollar energy company contacted my consulting company yesterday to do Information Security Penetration Testing on their company. Big $$$$$$$. I thank God for favor, many testimonies, peace, angels, miracles, blessings and more. I have lost count! God has opened up the windows of Heaven and poured out so much. I am OVER-FLOWING. I need help to take it all in!!

Apr 5, 2017, 6:19 AM

Some advice I can give to job-seekers is...

Pray & ask God for direction & have an ear that hears His response. Some know how to pray but don't know how to listen. You must know His voice, His personality and His presence.

Dec 25, 2017, 4:52 PM

I'm trying to stay humble and low-key in my profession while also standing for righteousness and being an advocate of honesty and truth through it ALL. NOW, elevation is happening very quickly without me volunteering. OTHERS are speaking on my behalf and volunteering and recommending me for highly impacting roles! Additionally, the Lord has been allowing me to be used as a door for others to be blessed. WOW!! AMAZING! HOW did I get here??! I am humbled. I love God and people.

Apr 19, 2018, 10:29 PM

How come our Mommies and Daddies can't just go to work and take care of our families without having to deal with the lustful behavior of men and women on the job? How would you feel if your daughter or son had to deal with your lustful behavior?

Sep 3, 2018, 8:33 AM

Thank you to everyone for the love, good thoughts and prayers in respect to my Cybersecurity Job-Readiness Training presentation held at the youth center. The training consisted of approximately 20 students (ages 12 - 18) and about 6 staff members. All in attendance seemed very interested, encouraged, motivated and inspired. I used multiple instructional strategies I had learned as a Davenport University Information Securities Professor, through Train the Trainer classes, performing as a technical trainer and so many more.

I felt that the combination of these training experiences, my passion to help others have a sustainable income in a very lucrative field and the blessings and mercies of God contributed to the presentation's success. I also provided the staff with a copy of the presentation outline, resources and a presentation survey for referral and follow-up purposes.

There was a lot of great feedback and they even clapped after the presentation. There is definitely more to come. God showed me this vision. I pursued it and will continue to pursue more opportunities such as these.

May 30, 2019, 11:29 AM

Dawn Kellum is feeling thankful.

...seeking God for wisdom, favor and understanding in areas of business caused $5451.87 of business debt to be completely forgiven within a month's time. Hope against hope. Stop stressing and seek God.

Jun 18, 2019, 6:08 PM

Message to all of my fellow Christian entrepreneurs: Ask God our Father for direction in all business matters and about every business move. I asked God about my family's business and He showed me in a vision where to go to get help with business planning, networking with similar businesses, funding sources, obtain employees and a beautiful office space for $400/month in the same office with a well-known company.

Do not love money or desire riches or you will fall into many temptations and possibly lose the faith. Love good business, Christian moral and ethical dealings, provide great services and love people like you love yourself or better than you love yourself. Move on God's timing. I cannot stress that enough.

While you are growing your business, live a simple personal lifestyle and not the high life, i.e., luxury apartments, big houses, fine cars, etc. Downgrade your high life as much as possible. Save. Save. Save. Use spiritual discernment given by the Holy Spirit. Love God and love people. Don't meet with people by yourself privately even if it is business. Be aware and ask God our Father to block anything He doesn't want for the situation at hand. I love you all and praying for you. Stay Blessed. I am sharing this in love.

Jul 13, 2019, 7:34 AM

God is so good. We are again so GRATEFUL for this opportunity. We have classes now accredited by US Homeland Security for training small businesses and responding to cyber incidents like hacks, data breaches, etc. Kellum Security Consulting also currently has students from 40+ countries, i.e., South Africa, India, Iran, United Kingdom and more so we also plan to expand some of our services globally. Other Federal Bureau of Prison training opportunities have also surfaced throughout the nation. This is bigger than what we thought. Let me know if you know anyone with international business knowledge and/or cyber Security experience.

Sep 28, 2019, 7:45 AM

I am going to see my first two patients in hospice care today to offer the gift of presence and administer music therapy. I solicit your prayers in our Savior's name.

Jan 23, 2020, 10:02 AM

Update: 1 of my hospice patients passed away today. I pray

that God will continue to comfort their family and all who loved him.

March 15, 2020

There are grant opportunities to businesses economically impacted by the pandemic. My company received $2,000.

Jun 19, 2020, 6:53 AM

Psalms Chapter 1

1 Blessed [fortunate, prosperous, and favored by God] is the man who does not walk in the counsel of the wicked [following their advice and example],

Nor stand in the path of sinners, Nor sit [down to rest] in the seat of the scornful (scoffers or ridiculers).

2 But his delight is in the law of the Lord, And on His law [His precepts and teachings] he [habitually] meditates day and night.

3 And he will be like a tree firmly planted [and fed] by streams of water,

Which yields its fruit in its season; Its leaf does not wither;

And in whatever he does, he prospers [and comes to maturity].

Oct 15, 2020, 10:01 PM

I LOVE this quote honoring C.S. Lewis...It is placed conveniently at the end of my emails at work and has been for a while now..

"I believe in Christianity as I believe that the sun has risen:

not only because I see it, but because by it I see everything else." - C. S. Lewis

Nov 23, 2013, 6:19 AM

When you surrender to God's will in your life & the favor of God is steering your life, nobody, no principality or power can move you from that position even if it's something you THINK you need. God wants you to know that HE is the one and true God. It is HE who loves you the most & will not allow any other power to be god over you. God is more than the world against you dear hearts. This reminds me of the song "He is jealous for me. His love is like a hurricane. I am like a tree. Oh how He loves us. Oh. Oh. How He loves us."

January 22, 2017

This is true. This will take a person a long way in life - ESPECIALLY a Christian. Too many people waste energy on combating attacks, false accusations, etc. instead of using that same energy to be productive. This is one of the main tenets I use and I have excelled in the workplace

Jun 6, 2013, 10:35 AM

When you are delivered up before men and angels — even in the context of an on-the-job decision — your ethical choice is your witness, so do not waver. If what you are being asked to do requires you to be disobedient to God, after having exhausted all questions and arguments to the contrary, stand firm. Make it clear that you can't do it, and you won't do it, as it would be a crime against your own God-informed conscience.

If you have the authority to make the right decision, use the authority and make the decision. When it's not your decision to make, speak into it, and if and when it goes down the other way, go to the Scriptures, go to prayer, and ask God whether you can remain in this job. God is your source. That job is a resource. Wherever God leads you He will surely take care of you. Don't love your ego, pride and money more than godly living. Who is your Father? God or satan?! Choose ye this day whom you will serve even if you have to take a pay cut. Eternal life with Jesus is far better than forever dying with Satan in the eternal Lake of fire.

Don't let it be just another little sin on your way to a "perp" walk, temporally or eternally. – taken from the Desiring God Facebook Page.

As I was cleaning and closing up at one of my jobs today, a thought came to my mind. I believe it had to have been a thought given by God. The thought was, "When you get finished building and reaching your financial goals with your business after investing much energy, time, money and more to invest in your family's future and support other financial endeavors, who is going to have that same zeal, vigor and level of passion to maintain and support those same financial goals??"

Feb 5, 2020, 3:34 PM

CHAPTER 10

God's Power to Heal and Deliver

Is any among you sick? Let him call for the elders of the church; and let them pray over him, anointing him with oil in the name of the Lord: and the prayer of faith shall save him that is sick, and the Lord shall raise him up. Confess your trespasses to one another, and pray for one another, that you may be healed (James 5:14-16).

May 20, 2014, 9:41 PM

Healed! I Thought I Wouldn't Sing Again

During June of 2015, I suffered a traumatic brain injury which progressively affected my ability to speak clearly and succinctly as well as sing. I experienced severe pain, major intracranial pressure and weakness when talking and singing. I developed a condition called speech aphasia where my speech was labored and my words were often expressed in a hesitating fashion. I had severe pain throughout my head that felt as if an ice pick was hitting different portions of my head.   The pressure in my head felt as if my head was going to explode. All of my other cognitive abilities, the ability to make decisions and physical/emotional abilities were fine.

Unable to Speak Clearly

The inability to speak clearly was devastating because I had to limit my speaking to a few sentences a day because the pressure and labor that occurred during speaking was almost unbearable. If I spoke too much, I felt weak and had to rest my head or take a nap just to relieve the pressure and because my body had gotten so weak. When I would talk or even attempt to sing, the pressure in my head increased the longer I spoke or tried to sing. My head felt as if it were a bicycle pump about to explode as the pressure increased.

Unable to Sing

I enjoyed singing praises to God. I loved to use my singing voice to praise God. I enjoyed feeling the presence of God while I entered into worship with Him through songs of thanksgiving, praise and adoration. I knew that God dwelled in the midst of the praises of His people. Worship to God through song breaks chains in a spiritual sense. Singing praises to God and worshiping Him helped me to have godly thoughts and swayed away ungodly and evil thoughts. It would change my atmosphere. In order to avoid arguing or getting upset, I sung praises to God and my whole perspective and mood would change for the better. When I was discouraged, I sung songs of praise that encouraged me and I would immediately start to feel better. I sung when I woke up, when I went to sleep, while I was at home , when I went to work, when I left work, when I went to church, when I left church and more. I enjoyed singing praises to God with and to my children, my husband, my family, loved ones and many more. I enjoyed encouraging others through song.

My inability to sing was the worst feeling I had ever felt in this world! When I lost the ability to express praise and worship to my God through song, my faith in God was shaken. I questioned God and asked, "God, why would you take the singing voice of a person who sings praises to you and worships you daily? God, please help me to understand." I cried daily and I felt almost hopeless.

Telling My Loved Ones

I tried as long as I possibly could to appear as if everything was fine to those around me. During one particular instance, and around the beginning stages of this horrible sickness, my sister asked me to sing for her graduation. I immediately responded with a resounding, "Yes! I would love to!" I love my sisters and would do almost anything for each of them. I was so proud of her academic achievements. When she contacted me, I was also suffering with bronchitis for which I had already had for about 2 weeks up until this point. The cough was horrible. I knew that it would be nearly impossible to sing with bronchitis so I prayed to God and asked Him to heal my body so I could sing for my sister's graduation. God healed my body that same day! The cough was completely gone within a matter of hours! God had healed me of the bronchitis; however, the pressure in my head was still there.

During the graduation I sung even through the massive pressure that permeated my entire body. I tried to limit my speech as much as possible. This was nearly impossible because much of my family was there and I wanted to speak to everyone. This was very difficult.

After a few days, the illness became worse. At that point, the pressure was worse and my ability to sing was nearly gone. People would still ask me to sing at different functions. I would push through the pain but be in agony once I left. I had a desire to sing; however, my body did not own up to it.

I finally gained the confidence and humility to express my situation to my friends, family and loved ones so they would be informed of my debilitating health. It hurt me to see them sad because of my failing health; however, I had to tell them.

My Road to Healing

I prayed a little bit above a whisper every day and throughout the day even through the tears and debilitation. It was a struggle to talk; however, I was persistent. I was determined to pray even if it hurt because I knew that prayer or communication with God was needful and changed situations around.

I also consulted and was referred to multiple physicians, neurologists, radiologists, therapists and more. They were able to come up with multiple reasons why I was sick; however, they could not heal me. I was left with more confusion and fear as well as an avalanche of unanswered questions and high medical bills. My faith in this present world's healthcare systems to heal me had diminished greatly. I knew that I had to increase my faith and confidence in God and trust in Him completely because no one else could help.

I knew that any healing would need to come from God. God was the source of my healing. God had healed me multiple times before and I knew that He could heal me this time as well.

I prayed to God, meditated on His word and took action to receive my healing based off of God's word, including, but not limited to, receiving prayer through the laying on of hands from my Big Sister "N" and my Pastor's wife. They are two very anointed women of God I look up to.

My Testimony!!

God healed my body and restored my ability to speak even clearer than before AND the ability to sing with an even greater eloquence unto His awesome glory. God anointed my voice with an even higher anointing than before. God gave me back more than what I asked for. I recorded my first FULL song in a cathedral in Cozumel, Mexico, Monday August 3, 2015 since I lost the ability to sing. That song was Amazing Grace. I have a recording of it on my website womenunspotted.com. It had to be recorded in order that God would get the glory for His healing power.

UPDATE June 2019!

I released a new single entitled We Will Sing June 2019. It is a song of triumph and victory rejoicing in God's faithfulness, mercy and love to miraculously heal me to sing again for Him. I believe that this song will inspire people around the world to never stop believing in miracles because they do happen. It is also an anointed song of praise dedicated to the glory of God and shows how deliverance comes through singing the praises of God in humble surrender to His divine will. My sister, Donna Grinstead and my son, Nahson Kellum assisted with background vocals with their 4-5-range vocals. Larry Trice III co-arranged the song along with myself. My cousin Rennard Stafford is on the drums. The song was recorded by GBP Productions USA and produced by Glenn Brown (Eminem, Kid Rock and more).

My music website, music Biography and more are found at www.dawnkellumsings.womenunspotted.com

Thank you God for allowing my body to be healed. I received confirmation from the doctor today. I don't need surgery or medicine. Praise God!

Jul 29, 2014, 9:03 PM

Dawn Kellum updated her status.

I thought about the following song when I suffered a traumatic brain injury that affected my ability to talk and sing:

Send a little help; let your angels fly, (fly)

Heard the words deep down inside,

I will survive,

I'm stronger cause I

I heard a word,

Saying, Girl you'll be fine,

I heard a word,

That would ease my troubled mind - "Heard a Word" - Michelle Williams

Jul 5, 2015, 7:44 AM

My family member suffered an illness that affected their ability to walk. They went to a healing service where Bishop

Winston Singleton of Los Angeles, California laid hands on them and prayed for them. They came back from the healing service walking! My God is amazing! Another family member who accompanied them said, "Dawn, look I gotta' show you something!!!"

Mar 5, 2016, 9:53 AM

..missed church service this morning. I still thank God for allowing me to be healed and giving the doctors wisdom on my further care. Do you not perceive it? GOD WILL make a way in the wilderness and rivers in the desert. Hallelujah!!

Jun 26, 2016, 1:04 PM

Dawn Kellum is feeling thankful.

I believe in miracles. As I sat in service listening to the sermon, I could feel an unseen force mending a very deep cut in my lip that came because of a horrible sickness. I believe that unseen force was the hand of God! Now I am sitting here smiling like I normally smile without my lip bleeding. Glory to God!! Faith comes by hearing AND hearing the WORD of GOD!! God thought that little old messed up me mattered. To God EVERYBODY matters!!

Jul 3, 2016, 8:38 PM

God healed me through the laying on of hands from a traumatic brain injury last year which affected my speech & ability to sing. God healed my hand a few years ago through the laying on of hands from a deep knife wound. God healed my leg years ago from a horrible bike-to-truck accident.

When you hear me sing, watch me play the keyboard or

watch me dance, you are seeing evidence of multiple healings. I am SO thankful because things could've gotten worse - BUT God.

Nov 30, 2016, 9:46 PM

Once my husband's eye patch was removed from his eye after eye surgery, he looked at me and said, "Honey, I can see! I can see!" The cloud over his eye which affected his ability to work and drive was gone. He is now back driving and working! Thank God for allowing the surgery to be successful with no infection or pain. Thank God for allowing my son to drive his Dad many miles back and forth to the surgery, follow-up care, etc. God will surely take care of you. Take nothing for granted!

December, 2020

My child's surgeon said this upcoming surgery will be his LAST surgery. Everything has evened out and is growing NORMAL. As a baby, multiple doctors said he would eventually end up in a wheelchair because of the rare bone disorder called hemihypertrophy. They also wanted to give him plastic surgery because of the facial deformity. Now he RUNS. He's NOT in a wheelchair and, now at 13 yrs old, he has grown to be a handsome young man. It is hard to tell he had ANY kind of deformity or disorder. Jesus Christ is LORD Hallelujah! Keep the faith. The prayers of the righteous availeth much. Never stop believing God. Don't give up.

May 21, 2017, 8:54 AM

TESTIMONIAL SERVICE IS NOW OPEN. OOOOH me me! Me first!!

My God is awesome. Last week during consecration I had pain out of this world AND while recovering from both the flu and bronchitis. I prayed and knew that God was with me no matter what I went through and if I never received healing in this life. I also stayed fasting with my church during consecration through it all until Thursday afternoon. Pain was everywhere and magnified throughout my entire body! I had very little sleep. It felt as if my entire body was being stabbed and beaten from the inside and out AND I had a heavy menstrual cycle.

I was on an inhaler for bronchitis nearly 7 times a day to help breathe. I had NO idea where the pain was coming from. The pain was so bad I had taken a dose of ibuprofen and that did very little for the pain. Last Thursday afternoon I went to urgent care wincing and crying in pain. They prescribed Neurontin! They also told me to follow-up with my doctor. The doctor didn't have an appointment until days later! I was terrified to take Neurontin because I knew my body couldn't handle something that strong. It would put me out of commission for days BUT I knew Communion was Friday and, as far as I can remember I ALWAYS receive healing or deliverance after communion.

I somehow knew I would get my healing!! I went to communion on no pain medication trusting God completely for healing. I also couldn't help but think about the pain that Jesus suffered and endured at the cross. My pain was nothing compared to His pain!! Thank you Jesus! During communion I worshipped the Lord and partook while remembering how

Jesus was crucified for the sins of the whole world. I felt the pain subsiding and by early Saturday morning it was completely gone!! My menstrual cycle even dried up before the scheduled time!

This week I had so much strength and energy to do all kinds of things and go to all kinds of places with NO pain and no pain medication and no need for the inhaler!!. Me and my family were well and healthy, running and jumping and enjoying ourselves!! Can't nobody do me like Jesus. He is my friend!! Hallelujah

Apr 6, 2018, 7:36 AM

"He Turned It!" Thank you God for allowing my child to be healed. The doctor confirmed results in blood work are now normal. Her and I were putting in the work to ensure a good healing environment for her body!! We weren't always successful. After a while, I just started praying for grace and for God to please have mercy on her. Her doctor smiled to her and said, "Consider this as a gift."

Oct 25, 2020, 9:17 AM

God will anoint you for the assignment He lead you to and bring healing for you to complete it. One morning I was playing the keys and leading a song about Heaven under the anointing of God with my church's band. I could barely breathe that same morning with diagnosed asthma symptoms, but God anointed me to sing to His glory.

When I was singing God gave me more wind to sing stronger and louder. God healed me to tell you in song that Jesus Christ, the Son of God the Father, is returning in the

Rapture. BE READY. Jesus loves us this we know. Those of us who know and love Jesus have a mansion in Heaven made just for us.

Mar 9, 2019, 7:17 AM

7 weapons to take back what was rightfully your inheritance in the name of Jesus Christ

1. The Name of Jesus. Philippians 2:9-11 (NKJV) Therefore God also has highly exalted Him and given Him the name which is above every name, 10 that at the name of Jesus every knee should bow, of those in heaven, and of those on earth, and of those under the earth, 11 and that every tongue should confess that Jesus Christ is Lord, to the glory of God the Father.
2. The Blood of Jesus Revelation 12:11 (NKJV) And they overcame him by the blood of the Lamb and by the word of their testimony, and they did not love their lives to the death.
3. The Word of God Jeremiah 23:29 (NKJV) "Is not My word like a fire?" says the Lord, "And like a hammer that breaks the rock in pieces?"
4. Speaking in Tongues Romans 8:26 (NKJV) Likewise the Spirit also helps in our weaknesses. For we do not know what we should pray for as we ought, but the Spirit Himself makes intercession for us with groanings which cannot be uttered.

5. Prayer Psalm 50:15 (NKJV) Call upon Me in the day of trouble; I will deliver you, and you shall glorify Me."

6. Praise and Worship 2 Chronicles 20:21-22 (NKJV) 21 And when he had consulted with the people, he appointed those who should sing to the Lord, and who should praise the beauty of holiness, as they went out before the army and were saying: "Praise the Lord, For His mercy endures forever." 22 Now when they began to sing and to praise, the Lord set ambushes against the people of Ammon, Moab, and Mount Seir, who had come against Judah; and they were defeated.

7. Pulling Down Strongholds 2 Corinthians 10:3-4 (NKJV) For though we walk in the flesh, we do not war according to the flesh. For the weapons of our warfare are not carnal but mighty in God for pulling down strongholds.

Oct 27, 2018, 7:49 AM

Ye shall lay hands on the sick and they shall recover. A loved one was horribly sick yesterday. I laid hands on them, anointing them in the name of Jesus Christ and asked our Father to heal them. They received immediate healing with no more sickness.

Mar 27, 2019, 7:13 AM

Dawn Kellum is feeling blessed.

Family, I was diagnosed with a severe middle ear infection last week. I had fullness in the ear and some hearing impairment for about a year and never really knew it was an ear infection until I started having severe, shooting ear pain last week. I went to the doctor and they gave me strong antibiotics because the ear infection was severe by then. I shared with the doctor my long-term symptoms and he confirmed that I had an ear infection the entire time! Well, I finished the antibiotics two days ago on June 18 and still had severe, shooting ear pain although I could hear better and the fullness in the ear had subsided.

Last evening I prayed while touching my ear and asked my heavenly Father to heal WHATEVER was going on with my ear. This morning when I was about to get my girls ready for summer camp, my ears opened A LOT and I have NOT had that severe, shooting pain! It went away! Now I can hear almost everything!! I hear the sound of birds chirping outside my windows when they are closed. I hear the sound of the wind on the road as I drive. I hear the distant laughter of my children in far rooms. I hear more sounds behind my head. The music being played in my car is at the lowest volume I have played in a long time. All I know is I once couldn't hear well and NOW I can AND the pain is gone.

Jun 20, 2019, 7:18 PM

Good Morning. When you all have time, please check out my new single We Will Sing. It is a testimony to God miraculously healing me with the ability to sing again after I suffered a traumatic brain injury June 2015 which affected my speech and ability to sing. It has blessed others and myself. God Bless you all.

Jun 23, 2019, 7:26 AM

God healed me multiple times before of other illnesses and I'm also going to trust Him to heal me again. The doctor's report has given me much to wrap my head around, but God has not given us the spirit of fear, but of love, power and of a sound mind. Please be kind and don't inquire about my condition. Please just say a prayer for me. I have a journey ahead.

Oct 9, 2019, 8:57 AM

My recent labs show the progression of illness reported to me by my doctor has significantly slowed by 99% within one month's time with no medicine. I'm thanking God in advance for complete healing, for the prayers of the righteous, my anointed church family laying hands on me for healing and my husband and children motivating and encouraging me. God also allowed me to come in contact with someone at my current school assignment that shared great wisdom with me concerning my health - a planned divine encounter. ALWAYS take God's leading even when you don't understand. Keep trusting God for your healing. Be encouraged. I love you all, although God loves you more.

Nov 12, 2019, 6:22 AM

I don't plead guilty or innocent. I plead the blood of Jesus Christ. I receive the blood of Jesus Christ which was shed for me. I receive the body of Jesus Christ that was broken for me. I plead the blood of Jesus as Jesus Christ is my portion.

Apr 12, 2020, 10:17 AM

Breaking generational curses and bad habits is tough because it requires you to go down a road less traveled or not traveled on at all. Just keep going as God leads you to victories.

Feb 26, 2020, 9:16 AM

Praise God. This miraculous story reminds me of when I was pregnant with my oldest daughter. I was starting to bleed and couldn't feel her moving for almost 2 days. The doctor and nurses just said to take it easy, rest, drink orange juice and wait. I prayed and asked God, "Is this pregnancy for naught?" He said, "No." I continued to pray and believe God and, approximately 2 days later she started moving again. Praise God. Then, a few months later, I gave birth to her after 9 miscarriages. This is the same daughter that looks just like my Mom and is now a healthy, beautiful, intelligent 12 year old. Never stop believing in God to perform miracles. He is the giver of life.

Dec 1, 2019, 9:21 AM

Good Morning. I completed the Martian half marathon race April 2019. This was my 3rd half-marathon since being diagnosed with heart failure nearly 15 years ago. It was a tough race, but I can do all things through Christ who continues to strengthen me. I believed God to take me to the finish line - 13.1 miles straight completed!! I believed God to give me the strength to make it to the goal and I did! I had the heart of a finisher.

To the ones waiting on your miracle, have the heart of a finisher and never stop believing God until you get your miracle. Keep pressing and moving in faith. It's not time to give up trusting God for your miracle. God is STILL working miracles!! Sometimes when we believe God for miracles, we have to humble ourselves, pray, seek His face, repent and turn from our ungodly and unholy ways. I had to do this a few times.

I believed God for MANY miracles. God has miraculously healed me from several illnesses and ailments throughout my life, including, but not limited to, a painful tumor on the back of my head from a rollover car accident that shrunk after prayer, regained ability to carry a child full term after 9 miscarriages, restored ability to talk and sing after a traumatic brain injury, healed of a severe ear infection that affected my ability to hear behind my head for nearly a year (medicine did not work), healed of severe migraines I endured for years, healed of a heavy menstrual flow I had since the age of 9, healed of acute bronchitis episodes I endured for nearly 20 years, healed of a severe leg injury I suffered after my bike ran into a truck, survived a heart attack with no heart damage and so much more. Trust God and believe. Be encouraged

Apr 1, 2020, 10:57 AM

MERCY!!!! I don't plead guilty or innocent. I plead the blood of Jesus Christ.

Apr 15, 2020, 7:02 AM

Testimony: "Healed on the way" - A little over a week ago I

injured one of my hands from applying too much pressure to a household item while cleaning. I could barely do anything with that hand, i.e. cook, write, lift, etc.

I prayed and asked my heavenly Father to please heal me because I need to be able to play the keyboard for praise and worship in a few days and to use my hand to function normally. I had increased compassion for those with no hands or who have limited mobility.

Glory to God! Hallelujah! I received my healing on the way to my big brother's home to work on the church's social media page. God is really showing me so much about Himself and His servants. The pain completely went away but ONLY AFTER BEING ON THE WAY TO WORK FOR JESUS. I am blessed beyond measure!

Jul 4, 2020, 6:39 AM

My family member was delivered from alcohol addiction almost 20 years ago. God is good.

Sep 7, 2020, 10:34 AM

My child had strep for the last 3 days. She was on the antibiotics and fever-reducing medicine; however, she was still very sick, weak and regurgitating. I barely slept for almost 2 days praying for her, monitoring her fevers even while taking care of other responsibilities around the house.

She started to recover but VERY slowly (Ref. scripture Mark 16:18 "You shall lay hands on the sick and they SHALL recover").

I thanked God in advance for healing her completely. I kept speaking life and complete healing on her behalf. Then yesterday, I prayed an EFFECTUAL, FERVENT prayer around my scheduled prayer time. I hadn't prayed a fervent prayer on her behalf like that since she had been sick; however, once I prayed that prayer, I could feel the BREAK-THROUGH in the spirit. A few MINUTES after the prayer, my husband and I noticed that she IMMEDIATELY started feeling better. She came to me and said "Mommy I'm Hungry" (tears). I got up and fixed her some food. She did NOT throw the food up. Praise God! This was the FIRST time she was able to eat without regurgitating. She also seemed more joyful and energetic. Hallelujah!

Then I went to another room to relax and catch up on some sleep until a few minutes later I heard what was like the voice of an angel singing in a very STRONG voice. She was sitting at the table singing the song "I Can Only Imagine." I sat there in amazement praising GOD (tears)! THEN she came to the room where I was and went over to my keyboard and, 'out-of-the-blue', STARTED PLAYING melodiously while singing the PRAISES OF GOD! She is only 6 years old! She was trying to play the keyboard at the same time as she sung. LOL! I don't remember her EVER trying to do that! She normally does NOT play the keyboard; but, she seemed INSPIRED to play it and sing at the same time like I normally do. The prayers of the righteous SURELY avail MUCH! Don't stop praying!

23 March, 2014 at 8:31 am

Praise Report: A friend of mine was very sick a few weeks ago. Her blood sugar levels were so high that she was going blind. I told her I would say a prayer for her. Well, I have been praying and fasting on her behalf and believing God for her complete healing as well as the healing of many others.

Fast forward. She told me today that she is doing much better and that her blood levels dropped from 30+ to 7+. She had A LOT of positive good health reports. Jesus Christ is the healer y'all. He allows our bodies to be healed. He loves ALL of us.

Feb 26, 2014, 6:36 PM

CHAPTER 11

God's Power to Reveal

I had a dream where many of my family members and our babies were all together in a kitchen either STARVING or eating junk food with 2 refrigerators FILLED WITH healthy food AND 2 working stoves. They were waiting for the keeper of the house to give permission to cook/eat the food!! Family, we need to put our resources together to help each other. Nobody should be starving, malnourished or going without basic needs.

Oct 18, 2017, 6:59 AM

I gave a warning from God to someone this week and the next day they got into a horrible situation where they barely escaped with their life. Please stop playing with God people.

Oct 29, 2015, 7:00 AM

Dawn Kellum was listening to The Lord Speaking to my spirit.

Be sober, clear-minded, watchful & alert in this season. Your enemy, the devil - like a roaring lion - is on the prowl looking for someone to devour. God will expose situations &

people's true motives in this season. God will make you watch & see the NOTICEABLE difference between right, wrong, good and bad. Keep your eyes open with sober-mindedness. Don't get caught up in the hype of the unreal. Do not be delusional. You will NEED to pray to God for clear direction and insight this season.

Jan 2, 2017, 11:52 AM

Pastor Minor preached on the topic "How to Weather the Storm".

Subtopic: 'Weathering the Storms of Life' taken from the biblical texts of Acts 7:54; Acts 8:1-17; Isaiah 32; Psalms 27:1-14 Sometimes God allows storms to come in our lives. Understand why the storm is coming. Storms come to expose us, to expose other people, to clean us up and to reveal what is under the surface of our hearts.

God wants us to know and understand Him. God wants someone to believe on Him and trust in His word. Realize that God is concerned about your soul and well-being. God doesn't want you to get caught up with the things of this world. Wear this world as a loose garment. The devil is the prince and the power of the air on the earth that we live on. People are disturbed and on edge because of things going on in the world. Know that there is a hiding place. That hiding place is in Jesus Christ.

Don't judge Jesus Christ when you know nothing about Him, have never tried Him or have allowed Him to work in your life. Give the Lord a chance. He will prove to you that He is 'I am that I am'. God wants someone to believe on Him and trust in His word.

Feb 26, 2017, 9:37 PM

We can point out others' faults and wrongdoing so quick and be blind as bats to our own. Reconnect my GPS (God-positioning signal) so the God of Heaven can shine the light on me to help me see ALL my faults and wrongdoing and give me wisdom on getting rid of them.

Sep 16, 2017, 9:07 AM

If we don't know the purpose of something then we use it the wrong way.

Jun 20, 2018, 8:02 PM

..reflecting on a vision the Father shared with me about a big move my family and I were going to make about a year ago the SAME night I asked Him what He wanted us to do. God revealed everything about that situation. We took heed and didn't make that big move. Who would have known months down the road the company I worked for would restrict us from transferring AND sold our division out to a company in another country?? GOD KNEW!

May 18, 2019, 7:55 AM

A Director at my job I worked at as a Cyber Security Engineer for a Critical Energy Infrastructure: "I appreciate all what you have done. You have been able to do impossible and very difficult things. I'm serious!"

Me: "You have to understand I have a higher power helping me. I have a God. MY God is my helper. I look to Him."

Sep 8, 2018, 5:51 AM

...when you are a shy introvert and still progress forward with a vision God showed you, so, because you trusted God, was patient and obedient, you continue to see the vision manifest. It is not what it looks like or what people or experts tell you can't be done. Please just trust what God said.

Aug 21, 2019, 11:38 AM

Trust God. I asked God to reveal the whereabouts of an individual I was concerned about and how they were doing. My Heavenly Father gave me a vision of their current status and the type of spirits they were around. I woke up and prayed about it and felt at peace. They called me this morning and confirmed the vision. I thank God for having peace. God knows all and sees all. He is the good Father.

Jun 7, 2019, 11:07 AM

...scary, scary, scary world we live in y'all. Why did my heavenly Father have to allow me to see that the ONLY person who came to the Online Protection seminar last night is one of many who should NOT be privy to the information in my Protect your Online Presence and Identity seminar - and he is not who he said he was!??

Thank God the presentation did NOT continue. Sometimes we wonder why things happen - even the newly rented projector wouldn't work right!! I know why now. WOW! This is so sinister what I just saw about this individual online. The Holy Spirit led me to research and how to research. This situation had to happen for my heavenly Father to show me that this seminar is ONLY for the vulnerable and NOT for the perpetrators!

God is my protector and I love Him so much, but He reveals SOOO much that it can be shocking at times. We don't always understand God's plans, but our Father in Heaven ALWAYS knows what is best for His children. Y'all better trust God, surrender to His will and allow Him to be Lord over your life so He can have His way in your life and help you like He helps me and many others. I also thank God that my son was there too AND he treated me to some dairy-free ice cream afterward. Y'all we gotta' stay prayerful and be really careful out here! Evil is real. Sometimes I ask God, "Why me?" and then I think about purpose and destiny and say, "Why not me?"

Jan 22, 2020, 10:35 AM

...when you set your eyes on a big money opportunity involving former colleagues, and your heavenly Father shows you why you shouldn't pursue it in a very vivid vision. Then, after the vision, your heavenly Father brings back to your remembrance specific conversations you've had with those former colleagues you had forgotten and/or blocked out. I almost slipped, but God!

Nov 5, 2019, 7:02 PM

Happy Friday! You are not running out of all options - just old, comfortable ones. Come out of old ways of thinking. Do you know how to recognize when God is doing something new in your life? How many signs does He have to send?

Nov 22, 2019, 6:30 AM

Happy Fabulous Friday: Be careful what you share to whom. Everybody is not rooting for your God-given vision or even invested in it. Some are predators who take advantage of people or just want to see how much money you're making so they can use you as a pawn in their web of deceit. Ask God to reveal to you what should be shared with whom. I asked my heavenly Father and He exposed a lot of predators and those praying for my downfall and many others intents. Trust God to ALWAYS tell you the truth. Thank you to all of you praying, rooting for and investing in my God-given visions. I have so much to share.

Sep 6, 2019, 8:43 AM

Be aware of the wolves in sheep clothing who are influenced by evil spirits and are serving up Satan's agenda or menu rather than the agenda of His Majesty our Lord and Savior Jesus Christ. You will know the wolves by their fruit and let God show you through His Holy Spirit in you.

Jul 15, 2020, 9:23 AM

It doesn't matter who betrayed you or lied on you. Don't turn your back on God. Run to Him and not away from Him. At times, God has to show us the ugly truth about situations and people; but, don't run away from Him because He exposed some stuff. Stay in God. Let Him comfort and enlighten you. Be engulfed in truth. Stay focused on God. Pray for those who hatefully use you and say all manner of evil against you falsely.

Aug 22, 2019, 4:27 PM

Dawn Kellum updated her status.

Who has the right eyeglass prescription to "read between the lines" into what is really going on in the world? Be not deceived.

Oct 3, 2020, 7:33 AM

..when God speaks, listen - even if it's something you don't want to hear. Don't be too quick to believe what people tell you. Listen to God. God is always right. Amen.

Nov 4, 2020, 9:05 AM

Happy "seeing the WHOLE truth" Friday! I prayed & asked the Lord to expose AND BRING to the light many things concerning A LOT of situations in my life. He DID THAT. Now, I pray for wisdom, instruction and divine intervention to FIX ALL OF THEM.

The man of God preached Sunday and said "EVERYTHING YOU NEED IS IN GOD'S HOUSE – EVERYTHING and EVERY ANSWER PERTAINING UNTO LIFE AND GODLINESS"

Dec 13, 2013, 7:21 AM

To all my friends, family and loved ones - be careful y'all. Everything is not always what it appears to be.

Nov 27, 2013, 4:56 PM

You don't need ears to figure people out. All you need is

eyes. Watch their actions and what kind of fruit they bring forth.

Matthew 7:17-18 (AMP) 17 Even so, every healthy tree bears good fruit, but the unhealthy tree bears bad fruit. 18 A good tree cannot bear bad fruit, nor can a bad tree bear good fruit.

Jul 7, 2013, 7:09 PM

CHAPTER 12

Visions and Spiritual Insight

Job 33:14 (AMP) : "For God speaks once,
And even twice, yet no one notices it [including you, Job].
15 "In a dream, a vision of the night [one may hear God's voice],
When deep sleep falls on men
While slumbering upon the bed,
16 Then He opens the ears of men
And seals their instruction,
17 That He may turn man aside from his conduct,
And keep him from pride;
18 He holds back his soul from the pit [of destruction],
And his life from passing over into Sheol (the nether world, the place of the dead).
Oct 10, 2020, 6:07 AM

Why my family didn't move to Florida
Congratulations! I was in process of finalizing plans to

move my family and I to Florida. My company was international and my husband and I often spoke up moving to Florida. I was so excited! I prayed to God, "Father, please show us where you want us to go." THAT SAME night I had a vision and this is how the Holy Spirit gave interpretation of it:

The SCENE: There was a conversation between a married woman (me), her husband and a charming old man. In the vision, I was the married woman.

Old man: "Hey. You're beautiful. You're smart. You're intelligent. I want you to come with me to this place where they can use your talent and your expertise."

Married woman (me): "Sure. This sounds good. Can my husband and children go?"

Old man: "They can't go this time. You are so smart and like a genius. They need YOUR talent and expertise. I will pay for everything you need."

Married woman (me): "Wow. Ok. Sure. No problem. Why not? Let's go. My husband shouldn't have a problem with it because this is for my career. I will just let my husband know."

Narration: Once I went on the trip, I returned to my husband and family. The old man continued to propose that I go on trips with him away from my husband. Slowly, the relationship between my husband and I started to fade away until the following happened:

Old man: "You are so beautiful, talented and intelligent. I really like you. I have two tickets for us to go to Cancun, Mexico."

Married woman (me): "I've always wanted to go to there and I've never flown a plane. I would love to go."

Narration: Suddenly, I came to my senses and realized that the old man wanted ME all this time.

Married woman (me): "Wait a minute. YOU aren't my husband. I want to go to Mexico, but not with you. I want to go with my husband. Where is my husband?"

Narration: I looked around and saw my husband afar standing in the church in the body of Christ looking in my direction waiting for me to come back and by that time I was out of the body of Christ with the old man and some other people FAR AWAY!!

Old man: "I assumed you weren't together because you were spending more time with me than with him. You wanted everything I had to offer! Now you don't want me! You tricked me! I want you!"

Married woman (me): "I never wanted you. I wanted the things you had to offer. Leave me alone. I don't want your trip. What me and my husband had is far better than anything you could ever offer me! We may not be living lavish or have a lot of riches, but I love him. I don't love you. Leave me alone. I don't want anything from you anymore. I want my husband! You wasted the time I could have been spending with MY husband. I'm going back to my husband in the body of Christ. You tricked me!"

Narration: The old man then disappeared and I went back to my husband.

Husband: "I've been waiting for you and praying that you come to your senses. I love you."

Married woman (me): "I'm so sorry. I apologize for making you feel alone and abandoning you. Please forgive me. I love you."

Husband: "I forgive you. I have always loved you and prayed you would make the right decision."

CONCLUSION: In the aforementioned dream, the husband represented or symbolized God as my first love and the husbandman. The charming old man was satan aka the devil aka the serpent aka the deceiver.

We should ask God for wisdom and discernment in EVERYTHING WE DO. God always leads us to where we need to be, not where we want to be. Turn off the world and pray to and hear from God. Are we willing to forsake riches, fame, houses, land, our career, jobs and more to do or stay in God's will? There are so many of us making plans trying to please people and/or fulfill the lusts or desires of the flesh when we should be placing God and His will first and foremost before anything else. If it is not in God's will at the time, cancel the plans. Obedience is better than sacrifice and to hearken is better than the fat of rams. God can see beyond what we can see. Only He knows the end from the beginning. Be not deceived. Listen to and take heed to God's direction.

If it's the Lord's will, we will go wherever or do whatever. God's will must be done firstly. We will seek first the kingdom of God and His righteousness and know that God will supply our every need and give increase. We surrender and bow to the will of God who orders our steps daily. Move to Florida in 6 months? Maybe. We will wait on God.

26 February, 2018

UPDATE!
A few months later after the Lord gave me this vision, our

company sold our division to a company in another country. Then we were instructed that we could NOT transfer to ANY other division, including, but not limited to, ALL divisions in Florida!!! Always seek God FIRST!!

God gave more insight on how the devil operates.

In the aforementioned vision, the husband represents God, the married woman is the Christian believer and the old man is satan aka the devil aka the snake aka the serpent.

The snake, as a symbol of satan the deceiver & accuser of the brethren, has wound its way around the human heart & filled us with its poison. The devil is trying to trick you and tempt you so he can devour or eat you. He wants to wrap himself around you, slither and lie to you.

Satan wants to sift you as wheat. Evil men make "their tongues as sharp as a serpent's; the poison of vipers is on their lips" of liars having venom or poison of a snake. Ask God for wisdom and discernment in EVERYTHING YOU DO. Get off your high horse. Turn off the world's noise and pray to and hear from God. Be not deceived.

Jesus Christ, the son of the living God, came into the world to crush the serpent's (the devil) head. Return to God who is your first love. Repent of your sins. Accept this great salvation through Christ Jesus. Use the word of God or bible scriptures to rebuke and cast the devil out and to gain wisdom. Receive Jesus Christ Holy Spirit. Jesus said that He had come to save us all from the serpent's bite "Jesus Christ must be lifted up so that everyone who believes may have eternal life in him" My feet almost slipped but Jesus Christ held me close. The Lord Jesus is our serpent-crusher. I'm a child of God.

Feb 18, 2018, 7:57 AM

Question: If you have a dream that someone will pass away, would you tell them? Personally, I would pray for them and seek the Lord for direction. If it's a warning, I try to get the message to them. In this post, I was referring to a vision of a family member who was committing ungodly sexual orgies. As they were having fun sinning, I looked afar at how close they were to death's door. They eventually became sick unto death, but repented and continues to serve Jesus.

Feb 23, 2015, 6:35 AM

I was headed to sleep with my telephone off until the front screen door started slamming on its own, sounds of things falling on its own, etc. I just felt unsettled. These things don't normally happen so I said a prayer.

After I prayed, God gave me a thought to turn my phone on. As soon as I turned it on, there were a LOT of messages. Someone was in an emergency situation.

Fast forward to a few minutes later. Now that the problem is being resolved, the door is not slamming anymore and it's quiet. Prayer Is Important.

May 7, 2014, 10:57 PM

I prayed until the wee hours of the morning asking God "Where am

I? Why am I feeling like this and much more!" He broke the chains in the spirit and gave me a breakthrough and the answers I've been seeking for a long time now. Some answers require you to go straight to the king! God is faithful. Seek and you shall find when you seek JUST HIM with ALL your heart.

Jan 6, 2015, 7:03 AM

...that moment when God allows you to see that the golden opportunity you're pursuing is an illusion and a trick, trap or pit from the adversary. Then you thank God for protecting you from it because you submitted to God's will and realized that His will is ONLY the BEST will for you.

Beloved, be not discouraged. Be strong in and through the Lord and His word. Praise God for exposing the deceit and trust Him to lead you to the BEST opportunity according to HIS will. God is real and wants you to have a bright future. Your life is in God's hands. NOTHING at all exists outside of God. Thank You God.

Oct 6, 2015, 7:12 AM

I had a dream yesterday of a place where many people were bowing. I did NOT bow just because everyone else was. I questioned WHO they were bowing to. Suddenly I stopped breathing in my sleep. Everything stopped! I managed to call the name of Jesus and IMMEDIATELY I started breathing again and awoke praising the Lord. My life is nonexistent without Jesus Christ. Bow Before The King.

Apr 24, 2016, 6:05 AM

I had a vision of my Mom praying even while in her weakened state and old age. She trusted and believed God through it all.

Mar 5, 2016, 10:29 AM

One of my children who also saw their grandma (in person) young & vibrant standing at her own gravesite just said they had a dream that their grandma (my Mom RIP) told them to tell us, "Be Ready" while pointing to the sky.

Apr 11, 2017, 7:15 AM

I dreamed of balls of light going across the sky. The Rapture was happening. People were looking at the news on their cell phones to confirm that's what it was instead of believing the promises of God and what they were actually seeing. I saw a minister's wife and another saint coming out of a hotel, consumed by the cares of this life and crying, "No! COME BACK TO LANSING TO GET US!" It was too late.

Oct 27, 2017, 8:04 AM

I had a dream that I was traveling going to and from busy with the cares of this world NOT in sin just BUSY. A lot was going on. I saw a place that had multiple funerals going on. I was doing daring feats. I wasn't sinning - just BUSY with the cares of this world. SUDDENLY I looked up and saw a man with chariots heading up into Heaven. I said, "HOLD ON. WAIT FOR ME. I'M SUPPOSED TO BE WITH YOU."

May 12, 2017, 7:02 AM

God is real. Trust the voice of God. He speaks through many different ways.

Jun 28, 2020, 8:40 AM

The anointing of God is what is needed. I remember God allowed me to hear believers, like my Aunt Adeline, who passed away, singing a song with HOLY in it in a very vivid vision in the presence of His Majesty. I was so comforted and encouraged by that anointed worship. I speak more about this vision in the chapter God of Comfort, Comfort Me.

Jul 13, 2020, 7:26 AM

I had a dream of a family member frantically telling me that they were planning a funeral. There was commotion and confusion in the house and the family member had lost a considerable amount of weight. I had NO idea that the family member was sick.

May 9, 2019, 5:32 AM

UPDATE! I eventually found out that the family member was very sick so I continued to pray, fast and consecrate on their behalf while speaking LIFE and praying for life in Jesus Christ name. The Lord also led me how to pray for the family member, their family, friends and others around her. Sadly, the family member passed away just a few months later. They were buried in the same outfit they had on in the vision. My heart was broken and my faith was shaken because I wanted them to live and I regretted not doing more for them and being in their life more.

Do you know how to hear from God?

Worship Him in Spirit and be true to who you are. Acknowledge your shortcomings and needs even though He already knows them. Confess them to HIM brothers and sisters in Christ. Your mind must become His mind. The word of God must become a part of you.

Your thoughts must become His thoughts. Whatever breaks his heart should break YOUR heart. Now, calm your spirit, open up your heart and be ready AND willing to receive the answer.

Bring down your high imaginations and worldly opinions. Bring every thought captive to the obedience of Christ Jesus AND then Listen. HE IS SPEAKING TO YOU NOW! Are you listening?

Oct 25, 2018, 6:00 PM

If that thing you seek is driven by bitterness, wrath, jealousy, greed, un-forgiveness, strife, to act ugly or to be spiteful, that SAME thing you seek will become UGLY to you. Do all things out of the love of God.

Oct 22, 2018, 8:02 AM

Dream/Vision November 30, 2018 - December 1, 2018: I see people coming to a church with ONE door and multiple levels that look the same. The greeter told the black people to go to one level, the white people to go to the other level, etc. The levels were filled from front to back with people according to the color of their skin.

Fast forward to real life: There was a Christian musical at a local church December 1, 2018. I saw hundreds of people of many nationalities and colors joined together in worship and praise to the King of Kings seated from front to back. Seated in front of us was a beautiful Caucasian couple lovingly protecting and nurturing an African-American baby who was quiet the entire time.

Insight: Do not have respecter of persons when it comes to Kingdom citizenship. There is only one door to salvation – through Jesus Christ. We all can receive salvation through Jesus Christ. It doesn't matter what your skin color is. Don't be ashamed of your skin color when you are fellowshipping with people of other skin color types. God is masterfully colorful and outstandingly beautiful and we are all his offspring - although made in the image of Adam as a fractured creation because Adam sinned; but, when we received Jesus Christ as Lord and Savior, we are now, spiritually, in the image of God and adopted into the Kingdom of God's dear son. We are ALL brothers and sisters in Christ – no matter the color of our skin. The blood of Jesus Christ runs warm in the veins of all those who have received Him as their Lord and Savior. We can still fellowship together. Oh how good and pleasant it is for brethren to dwell together in unity.

Dec 2, 2018, 9:39 AM

A family member was having issues in school. The parents were repeatedly contacted. Eventually, the family member was suspended from school for dragging a girl across the concrete. I sought the Lord about the situation and I asked my Heavenly Father to reveal the situation to me.

Vision: In the vision was the family member and the girl who was dragged. When the administration was not looking, the girl would tell the family member to do dastardly deeds, curse at the family member and act horrible. Once the administration would come around, the girl would change up and tell on the family member. This happened repeatedly.

Update! The family member was amazed I knew specific details like the specific curse word combinations and more that they didn't share with me concerning the situation; but, our Father knows and sees ALL - not just what we want people to know. God has our BEST interest at heart. God is real. Eventually, the family member went into behavioral counseling and was removed from the school by the parent and, after much spiritual direction, attending home school and Christian school for a few months, the family member returned to the SAME school with NO problems WHATSOEVER!

May 13, 2019, 9:00 PM

...when I ask my heavenly Father for direction and He leads me to a solution or strategy AND/OR gives me very vivid visions on where to go and how to proceed and what type of spirits are involved - not always the actual people. God's direction is ALWAYS on point.

May 16, 2019, 7:56 AM

My company got asked to do a Cybersecurity Job Readiness presentation/training next week to youth at the youth center. This was another confirmation from a vision my heavenly Father gave me for my company.

May 23, 2019, 10:38 AM

Happy Friday family. Ask the Father to reveal to you what He wants you to be doing now. He shared at least two things with me in a vision, when, after pursuing them, the DOORS WERE ALREADY THERE FOR ME TO WALK INTO. NOBODY has ever shared these things with me.

MORAL OF THE STORY: Sometimes you have to go to God for yourself for your destiny. GOD does not always share what He wants you to do with other people. Stop stressing and just pray and trust God.

May 17, 2019, 7:17 AM

Family, I am still in awe from yesterday until today. I asked my Heavenly Father weeks ago what HE wants me to be doing in my business. He gave me a vision the same night I asked Him weeks ago. Well, some of it was made manifest weeks ago and a large part of the vision was manifest between yesterday and today from where to go, what the person would look like, the path to get there and so much more. Now, when I got there, the individual there appeared to be in shock and amazement. They made a statement with a big smile and said, "It is rare that a minority is doing this. There is SO much help for you and there is your office and these are the people who will help you and we have people that will work for you and so much more!"

What!? God. My God. My Father is holding and directing me y'all (TEARS) and making sure I do what HE wants me to do. He has even prevented ME from getting other opportunities over the past few weeks to ensure I ONLY do what He wants me to do with NO wavering at all.

After today, my faith is now even stronger. The vision He showed me is coming to pass. Trust God family! He also blessed my husband with TWO jobs within the past 2 weeks. He was contacted immediately for both and got hired at the interviews. He ultimately chose one. God is so good to me y'all. I just can't thank Him enough!! Trust God family. Keep a good relationship with our heavenly Father and just trust Him and stand on His promises. When you feel like your faith is wavering, just hold on a little while longer. He has made so many ways for me, my family, my loved ones and more from healing to deliverance to breakthroughs and more. What God has promised you, HE will do!! Be Encouraged. Ain't no need to worry what the night is gonna bring. Talk to God and just trust Him.

Jun 28, 2019, 10:11 PM

Following a vision that God gave me, I went to the location God showed me and talked to the people God showed me and scheduled a formal meeting with them. When my husband and I attended the meeting, they took us into a room and kept asking in wonder, "How did you find us?" or "How did you hear about us?!" I didn't tell them that God sent me and that my relationship with God got me what your influential network got you. They proceeded to say, "We are here to help you with anything your company needs. Anything. We have only one space available here at this location for your company." This blew our mind. And someone paid one of my family's big personal bills today!! The list goes on and on! Just trust God y'all!

Jul 9, 2019, 6:29 PM

I had another vision and, to make a long story short, it's time to get into the ark of safety with Jesus because the doors are about to be closed. Now, they are in process of closing.

Aug 5, 2019, 7:45 PM

BROTHER/SISTER EAGER: God showed me these visions and I will make them come to pass. I'm tired of waiting. I see those around me making strides and doing some things. It's time for me to MOVE. It's time for me to MAKE it happen no matter what!

GOD: Wait. Trust me. Wait on me to tell you when to move and it will all manifest in my timing - the BEST timing. There are critical steps you must take in the process before each vision manifests. You must learn how to listen and follow instructions well. Do not make hasty decisions. Allow me to lead and you follow me. Be not discouraged because you don't see what I showed you yet. Create an altar of praise while you wait. Encourage others while you wait. Work for the kingdom while you wait. Trust the process of the Sovereign God. If God said it, you believe it. If God said it, that settles it. If God said it, you look for it; but, trust divine process and listen to me for the next move. Be encouraged. Hope thou in God. There will be an expected outcome.

Jul 20, 2019, 7:35 AM

Hey Family. My company was provided a new office space in East Lansing, MI as of August 1, 2019. This is the place God showed me how to get to in a vision some weeks ago. God also showed me in that same vision the people and places to go through to get it with NO charge to me or my company. God also showed me where to get the help to ensure the success of my company. Also, since my company started in 2016, about 220+ students have been trained in Cyber Security. I love what I do.

Aug 17, 2019, 5:28 PM

February 5, 2021 UPDATE! There are currently about 10,000 students being taught my me worldwide as of today.

When God gives a vision, God will send who He wants to help support it. Sometimes they are not in your "circle." You're waiting for the vision to manifest but refuse to go to who God says go to for the next level of manifestation. You're knocking on the wrong door when you know what door He said to go to. That door may not have family or friends or your own resources and means written on it.

Lean not unto your own understanding. He is showing you something amazing. Don't be angry with God or your family and friends because you were disobedient. Love God and Your loved ones. This is between you and God at this point.

Your anger and stubbornness doesn't change God's mind about the door He wants to use to bless you or when He will open the door. Have we learned anything from Jonah and Job in the bible? Trust God's will and His process. His ways and thoughts are far above our thoughts. If He wants to deliver you in what you see is the worst of it and give you peace, then receive His deliverance and peace during this time until the vision manifests.

Sep 21, 2019, 5:55 PM

I love how my heavenly Father shows me events, situations, conversations and more before they happen to prepare me for whatever, comfort me, and/or, in some cases, warn me. Who wouldn't want to serve a God like this?

Oct 27, 2019, 7:37 AM

Good Morning Family. What would you do if you looked at someone walking towards you and saw their face on the outside and another non-human strange looking entity inside of them AND both were looking at you? I rebuked the devil in them in the name of Jesus Christ.

Oct 19, 2019, 11:26 AM

When you have Jesus Christ's Holy Spirit, you have power to see everything through the eyes of the one who gave you the Holy Spirit.

Nov 23, 2019, 7:49 AM

My heavenly Father shows me a lot of very vivid visions. Here is another one.

Vision Scene: A Church

Narration: I watched from afar. There was a church member seated in the front of the church waiting to hear a word from God and needing a healing. There were other people in the church playing around and not taking the word of God serious. There was a man and a lady committing ungodly sexual acts with each other in the church. The preacher would occasionally stop the sermon to bring order in the church; however, after order was temporarily brought to the church, the unruly individuals continued playing in church and committing ungodly acts inside the church. Still, the lady seated up front was not distracted, but sat there intently awaiting a word from God and needing a healing.

The Message: "Don't waste ALL your valuable kingdom business time rebuking the tares and the "Judases" (fail to be discipled by Christ). Bring forth the word of God. Lay hands on the sick and they shall recover. Fulfill the work of the ministry God has called you to do. Be obedient to God. Visit the sick. Clothe the naked. Help the widows and the fatherless. Feed the hungry buffet style. The "wheat" need a word and a healing. More people are coming into the church to be saved. Stop allowing the "tares" to distract you." The table is spread and the feast of the Lord is going on. Receive all what God has for you. In the end, Jesus will separate the wheat from the tares. The tares will be cast into outer darkness. The wheat will have eternal life with Jesus Christ forever.

Update: I remember leading a song, "Deliver Me" at my church and, on one part of the song where great emotion was given, I looked at the same individual God showed me in the vision who was seated in the front of the church needing a word and a healing. As I looked into their eyes, I felt great compassion with tears all the while praying earnestly in my spirit and wailing, "LOOOOOOORD. Deliver Me!"

Nov 2, 2019, 7:28 AM

Update! The person referenced in the aforementioned awaiting a healing has since healed and recovered from a grave illness. They are doing well. To God be the glory.

I had to share. God will provide. I encourage you to trust Him. An unannounced stranger stopped at the door today to give specifically what I had just prayed to the Lord about. Also, over the past few weeks our kids were given $200+ in gift cards and other gifts from multiple strangers without us asking them for it. SO many other prayers prayed have been answered as well. Plus, the Lord gave me a vision of my sister "D" yesterday that has given me much peace and direction on what more I need to pray for concerning her.

God also takes me on vacations in visions where I wake up rested, encouraged, inspired and so much more. One night with the King can literally change your outlook on things. He has also given me greater insight and visions concerning much. I know when He gives the vision vs other sources. I have learned His voice and His presence. God is true to His word. Seek His face. I boast in the Lord's goodness. Whenever we fall short our Father meets us wherever we are to fill in the remainder - whether we know what that remainder is or not. Even when we don't know what to pray for, the Holy Ghost maketh intercession with groanings that cannot be uttered. Be encouraged.

Jan 1, 2020, 7:47 PM

Visions and dreams: I rested last evening with a thankful heart of surrender to a faithful and loving God who always has my best interest at heart. My loving Heavenly Father showed me a vision of young people out riding their bikes at night in a neighborhood. Some appeared to disappear. It was hard to see what was going on due to the darkness of night until I said, "I have a hard time seeing." Suddenly, my Heavenly Father exalted me high above the trees at His view. Immediately it was like daytime and very bright outside. He asked me to turn around. I saw all the children and many others outside. Every individual could be seen clearly and nobody was hidden at all.

Life Lesson Takeaway: We, as humans, may not be able to see everything, but God knows all and sees all. Nothing is hid in His sight. I meditated on this and the Lord showed me the scripture that says "Nothing in all creation is hidden from God's sight. Everything is uncovered and laid bare before the eyes of him to whom we must give account" (Hebrews 4:13)

Dr Billy Graham said, "We are limited in our knowledge — but God isn't. We are imperfect — but God isn't. We don't know the future — but God does. We don't even understand ourselves or our motives sometimes — but He knows all about them."

Dec 6, 2019, 8:50 AM

...listening to my automatic anointed shuffle of 459 songs

and bible scriptures from my phone. It doesn't matter where I start the shuffle, an inspirational scripture or song will come on speaking directly to whatever I'm thinking or going through or to the present situation at hand. This happens in the workplace, spending time with loved ones, etc. Here was a shuffle phase Christmas Eve 2019. God speaks to us through many ways.

I Tim 5, song So Good, John 1, Hebrews 10, John 15, Romans 8, song I almost let go, song Fresh Oil by Lisa Martin, Rev 20, song Undeniable, Luke 24

Dec 24, 2019, 8:30 PM

Don't get caught up in the hype of the unreal. Do not be delusional. You will NEED to pray to God for clear direction and insight this season.

Jan 10, 2020, 8:34 AM

Sometime before Christmas 2019, my Heavenly Father gave me a vision of a lot of people giving me 250 of something. I didn't know what it was but I kept expecting it. Well, the entire unsolicited gift cards my family and I received over Christmastime from random strangers and some friends totaled $250.

Jan 15, 2020, 6:28 AM

I had a dream some time ago about being in a hospital room and lying on a hospital bed under a huge thick blanket. There were multiple hospital staff in the room holding multiple tools. They were dressed in gear used when performing surgeries, like surgical gowns, masks, hair coverings and more. They were trying to operate and/or do their procedures on me; but what appeared to be BUTTERFLIES were flying ALL around them, me and all over the room and getting in the way of successfully completing the procedures. There were butterflies of all sizes in the room flying everywhere! I then stepped back from being in the bed to looking afar at what was going on. I noticed that there was a person lying in the bed with a thick blanket. Their eyes kept looking at me intently even while the butterflies (big and small) kept preventing the tools from working effectively.

Fast forward to April 2020. God brought the strange dream back to my remembrance that made NO sense when I experienced it. The world is now experiencing a pandemic or pestilence in the form of Covid-19.

Could the huge, thick blanket represent warming someone up who has a high fever? Were the medical staff dressed in PPE (Personal Protection Equipment)? Could the butterflies represent the virus and how it operates? Could the challenging procedures in the dream represent why it sometimes takes days to treat the potentially fatal viral pneumonia because the presence of "butterflies" is so thick? Why were some butterflies big and others small?

Apr 3, 2020, 8:15 AM

Update: The aforementioned vision was about a loved one who succumbed to Covid-19. The butterflies represented the Covid-19 viral load. No matter how much oxygen was given to the loved one from the machine, the oxygen couldn't get to the organs as needed. They eventually became non-responsive and, upon visitation days before they succumbed, their eyes would glare intently at me through the glass. The color of the blanket represented the color of their casket. Butterflies also represent resurrection and new life. I later had a vision of them rejoicing and walking out of the hospital in a new body. To be absent from the body is to be present with the Lord.

I must be truthful. My eye burst a blood vessel when I didn't want to go to sleep because God was showing me more vivid visions of people, places, the world, the afterlife and so much more. Please pray that I will continue to yield to my heavenly Father's will. This is a heavy gift.

Jul 1, 2020, 8:45 AM

Dawn Kellum is feeling thankful.

I remember a few months before my Dad and Sister passed due to Covid complications, God showed me a vision of me standing in front of a cemetery. My pastor Bishop Singleton (representing himself and the church) was at my left hand consistently handing me things. My Cousin Katrina was at my right hand standing looking at me.

Fast forward to August 2020 - approximately 3 months after my Sister and Dad passed. The vision God showed me was on point because my Pastor and church family have consistently shown my entire family and I love in so many ways before and since my Dad and Sister died in May of this year

2020. They have been there with presence and presents, at both memorials, offered prophetic guidance through divinely prophetic anointing, offered prayers on our behalf, given and offered grief counseling, given words of comfort and so much more!

My Cousin Katrina has been at my right hand both physically and spiritually during this very traumatic journey. She was at right arms standing in front of my sister's casket at her viewing guiding people as they viewed the body (she volunteered). She was there standing at my right hand holding and speaking to me when I fell to the ground and lost it at my Dad's memorial service and never left my side during the entire service (again showing love just because). She was at my right hand taking temperatures and asking about symptoms as I reentered my church's building for the 1st time since the pandemic.

God also showed me a vision last year, in 2019, of people with masks on inside my brother's house, whose new house I hadn't even visited yet. He opened up his house for family to gather there during my Sister and Dad's last days on this earth. It is amazing when God shows you far ahead in advance the ones He will use to bless you.

Thank you all so much for the genuine love. God saw it before it happened and showed me. God saw your love before you showed it with your actions. God is amazing.

Aug 30, 2020, 9:41 AM

I've learned the voice of the Lord. It's wonderful to have a relationship with Jesus Christ.

Sep 11, 2020, 7:42 AM

..when you experience in a dream a Sermon on a stone mountain with stones as seats and people dressed as they did during Jesus' time on this earth before His crucifixion. I saw one family where a younger child was carrying a long-handled bowl as they walked away. Also, I would come to the sermon location and return to go sow into the kingdom. Bishop LW Gates was present in the vision too. What an experience to sit at Jesus feet!

Oct 4, 2020, 8:03 AM

ALWAYS LISTEN TO GOD. My child's school computer has not been broken during this entire virtual school experience. Well, I walked past their room a couple days ago and saw the laptop. The Lord immediately spoke to me and said, "The laptop is broken." I was thinking, "Why wouldn't my child tell me it was broken so I can fix it or drop it off to be fixed??!!" Nothing on the laptop appeared to be broken. I didn't immediately follow up because I just KNEW my child would have told me something SO important so I disregarded God's warning.

Fast forward to Monday morning. I encourage my child to get online so they're prepared before class starts to ensure everything is okay. She said, "The laptop is broke." She knew it was broken a couple days ago but was afraid to tell me. Thankfully, I had an extra laptop of mine for her to use and everything was fine. God is always right! Learn His voice, listen to Him and take the necessary actions. God loves you.

Oct 26, 2020, 9:01 AM

Good Morning and Happy Friday FBF. I love to sing the song, "I'm so glad Jesus lifted me" because Jesus Christ gave me a vision years ago of Him snatching my soul out of Hell once I gave my life to Him and repented of my horrible and forbidden sins.

Now it's time to PROVE to Jesus Christ that I want Him more than anyone and anything else and that I am GRATEFUL and THANKFUL and GLAD He set me free, He lifted me and He MADE me see the truth.

Feb 21, 2014, 10:17 AM

I had an abortion in 1998 at approximately 5 weeks gestation. I never had the opportunity to know the sex of the child – whether male or female; but, I had a vision January 8, 2021 of the child I regretfully aborted. In the vision I was in a church-like setting. I then heard that familiar voice of a Loving Savior I would hear often in prophetic visions. I am very emotional as I write this. The voice said, "This is your child." I said, "What child?" I then briefly glanced over to my right and saw a young, fine, medium-brown skinned African-American gentleman sitting there with a hurt look on his face looking straight ahead and not directly at me. I responded, "That's not my child." The young man started crying. The voice of a Loving Savior responded and said, "He is 21." It then occurred to me that this fine young man WAS the CHILD I ABORTED IN 1998. I then looked toward the young man sitting there. I immediately hugged him and embraced him and repeatedly said, "I am so sorry!" All I felt was the peace and love of God.

Once I awakened, I calculated the years and months and, the child I regretfully aborted, would have indeed been 21. Please do not ask me why I stopped counting the years. I just did. Please just pray for me. I live with this pain everyday. My child lives and is with our loving Savior. One day I believe I shall be reunited with him and all of the 9 children I lost through miscarriage. They are with Jesus and He is taking good care of them.

Sunday October 18 2020

I recently witnessed a "Joseph and his brothers" moment – Ref. Genesis 37:3

I had a vision of a person threatening and taunting me constantly and I and someone else killed them by busting their head wide open. I told the other person to hit them over the head (murder accessory). Then we tried to hide the body, the bloody shirt, their phone and other things. No matter where I went, I could see the law enforcer speaking to me, "I will find you." Eventually, the law enforcer found the phone and the shirt. The phone was found on the road. I also saw eyes in the sky watching my every move.

Insight: If you hate your brother or sister in Christ with or without what you see as just cause, then you are a murderer who has committed a heinous crime and tried to hide the evidence. Be sure of this that God is watching from above and your sins (evidence of the murder) will find you out. Turn yourself in. Be convicted by the Holy Spirit. Repent.

Last modified: Oct 18, 2020

Vision and Insight: November 17, 2020

Why are you sitting on that couch with your legs gapped open showing your purple underwear while the minister is bringing forth the word? The woman of God approaches the woman on the couch and says in a kind, sweet and loving voice, "You don't want anyone to lose their job do you?."

Last modified: Nov 18, 2020

When God Speaks: A few days ago the Lord spoke to me in a vision and said the employer (either my job or my husband's job) would give towards our rent for one month AND another month. Well, my husband told me yesterday that his job is giving him a huge holiday stipend for this month and next month - November and December.

At last night's Called Women's Conference, Lady Singleton said, "When God promises, it will come to pass." Hallelujah!

Last modified: Nov 14, 2020

Don't worry about what others think woman of God. Focus on helping people who need it and not the ones treating you bad and not supporting. My company gets more help from God sending me signs, giving discernment, vivid visions to warn and/or prepare and the people who will help to do what, etc. Recently, God showed me another saint with a similar vision to the one God gave me.

Don't focus on the ones who are not supporting or help-ing. They will only distract you and waste a lot of valuable time you could be using to teach somebody a new skill to help them support their families. Jesus is the Savior of the whole world. The world frowned and still is frowning on him. Just because something is popular and praised by this world - it does not mean it's always good anyway. Understand also that people are fickle too and can't always be trusted. Many of your friends are jealous of you because they want what you have and can't.

Also, if you let the people build you; they will also tear you down. Your foundation must stand on something deeper than people's opinions. Keep shooting the baskets with or without the applause; with or without the hecklers and hat-ing. Continue to be righteous and moral through it all. Seek God continuously for direction. I applaud you for helping people to take care of their families. Their children will be grateful you helped their parents. BE ENCOURAGED.

Last modified: Nov 5, 2019

In my relationship with God, I learned the following and am a witness to these things as I walk in divine purpose. I hope these encourage you all as well.

1. You don't always have to fight for entry to the door God has already given you access to because God fought on your behalf and already created a way. Fight

through prayer only and move strategically according to Romans 8:14. He will give you everything you need behind every door He opens for you. Can you see it through the eyes of faith? Can you hear God speaking? Can you hear the door opening? One of my Daddy's favorite songs was, "The door is open. Walk in." by Eddie Robinson

2. Enemies are entities, demons, evil spirits operating in people, places, things, objects and/or are against the plans and purposes of God Almighty in your life.

3. As you continue to walk in divine purpose, God has justified you and Jehovah Nissi has raised a banner up so you don't have to figure out who your enemy is or what the enemy is conspiring behind your back because God is fighting on your behalf and will show you your enemies and their detailed communications and plans against You. You will get your answers in the War or Prayer Room and even in night visions and more. Let God show you many wondrous and amazing things. He will give you wisdom to deal with the enemy's tactics although it may hurt you to find out who is being used by the devil and his employees. Remember the devil is a liar and let God be true/truth and every man a liar. God never lies. Receive the truth and every man a liar. God never lies. Receive the truth He shows you and let Him take all your hurt, tears, heartbreak, unforgiveness and more. If you don't forgive those who sin - even heinous, disrespectful crimes - against you, your Father in Heaven will not forgive you your trespasses against His Majesty. Be aware also that many

have evil spirits in them causing them to refuse divine correction for their wrongdoings, heaping to themselves teachers having itching ears, becoming demonic hotels, denying the faith and the great commission of Jesus Christ, turning their backs on God and hating God's plans in your life. Pray for those who hatefully use you and say all manner of evil against you falsely, but forgive them first. God loves you.

4. Continue to trust God loved ones. Be encouraged. I love you all but God loves you more.

Jul 14, 2020

CHAPTER 13

Love and Forgiveness

Dawn Kellum updated her status.

"But to you who are listening I say: Love your enemies, do good to those who hate you, 28 bless those who curse you, pray for those who mistreat you." Luke 6:27-36 (NIV) 27

Oct 31, 2014, 6:19 AM

I choose to forgive the inexcusable so God will forgive the inexcusable in me. Forgiveness Is A Choice Of Justness By You And God.

Apr 2, 2014, 5:40 AM

Forgiveness: Jesus said if you don't forgive those who trespass against you, He will not forgive you your trespasses against HIM Matthew 6:14-15

Apr 26, 2014, 8:19 AM

Good Morning. "The most wonderful places to be in the

world are in someone's thoughts, someone's prayers and in someone's heart" - Patricia Polacco

TO ALL: YOU are in my good thoughts, prayers and in my heart. Have a Blessed Day!

May 4, 2014, 9:21 AM

(tears) I remember my sister drove around all night looking for me to find me sitting on the ground outside of a homeless shelter waiting to be transported to the night homeless shelter.

Apr 29, 2014, 8:19 PM

If we claim to be in the light and hate someone, we are still in the dark. (CEV)

1 John 2:9 This was in reference to bullying and cyberbullying.

May 8, 2014, 11:24 PM

Good Morning. Don't forget to show love to someone else. Everybody needs to experience love and compassion. God Is Love.

May 17, 2014, 7:41 AM

If I say I love God and don't love you, I am a liar. If you say you love God and don't love me, you are a liar. Ref. I Corinthians 13:4-8

May 22, 2014, 7:06 AM

If you treat people the way they treat you, then you are letting them be your god or your guide. If you treat others the way YOU want to be treated you are letting God be your God and your guide

May 30, 2015, 8:55 AM

Dawn Kellum was watching The Love of God FLOW.

I am thankful to God for allowing me to see MORE and more that He TRULY loves EVERYBODY and so should I. GOD is LOVE. I should represent His LOVE because He is the Greatest Love of All. Love is of God. They that loveth are born of God .

Nov 20, 2014, 10:32 PM

Dawn Kellum is feeling inspired.

Happy Sunday. Everybody is important. Look out for people even if you don't think they're worth your time. Matt 25:45 (GWT) "He will answer them, 'I can guarantee this truth: Whatever you failed to do for one of my brothers or sisters, no matter how unimportant they seemed, you failed to do for me.'

Feb 15, 2015, 7:11 AM

Follow peace with all men and never let your love wax cold.

Oct 24, 2017, 6:55 PM

...not my job to judge anyone - just love like my God says to love.

Jun 28, 2015, 7:30 AM

"It is the Holy Spirit's job to convict, God's job to judge and my job to love." - Billy Graham

Jun 28, 2015, 7:35 AM

Choose the love of God over hate. It is the merciful who shall obtain mercy. Let those who have no sin cast the first stone.

Mar 16, 2016, 7:01 AM

This is for those who don't want to travel to see their loved ones because their loved ones rarely, if at all, travel to see them. If it's the Lord's will, travel to see them anyway. Your blessing is in the travel not just at the destination. You will understand this once you're on your way. God bless you.

Nov 15, 2016, 7:17 AM

Remember the man named Job in the bible? His captivity was turned as he took all of his attention off the problem and prayed and interceded for his legalistic, over-spiritual, judgmental friends who had NO clue what God was doing in Job's situation. The one who needs intercession SOME-TIMES becomes the intercessor.

Jul 26, 2017, 10:01 AM

...that moment my neighbor scares the living breath out of me after running frantically to my car to thank me for sliding her daughter's income tax check and payroll check under their door after the mailman/mailwoman mistakenly put them in my mailbox. How did she know it was me?! Treat people how you want to be treated. What would Jesus do?

May 10, 2017, 8:08 PM

Take notes of those people who love you even when you have nothing else to offer them but yourself. Some people have ulterior motives and always want benefits like you're their employer. Some will never just love YOU.

Aug 9, 2017, 7:40 AM

Remember that the one you chose not to help or even pray for has the same God as you who knows and sees all. Love everybody.

Sep 4, 2017, 9:57 AM

Love vs Lust - If you're in love, the attitude of your heart is one of selflessness with the other person as your focus. If you are in lust the attitude of your heart will be one of selfishness, with yourself as the focus.

True love is driven by a godly desire to provide for, nurture and care for the other persons needs.

Lust is driven by an ungodly desire to provide for, nurture and care for OUR own sinful passions. When you lust after someone, you get angry and throw in the towel as soon as you don't get what you want, or you manipulate them until they do what you want them to do.

Aug 11, 2017, 8:21 AM

Ephesians 4:32 Be kind to one another, tender-hearted,

forgiving each other, just as God in Christ also has forgiven you. Acts 28:2 The natives showed us extraordinary kindness; for because of the rain that had set in and because of the cold, they kindled a fire and received us all. Acts 14:17 and yet He did not leave Himself without witness, in that He did good and gave you rains from heaven and fruitful seasons, satisfying your hearts with food and gladness." Hebrews 6:10 For God is not unjust so as to forget your work and the love which you have shown toward His name, in having ministered and in still ministering to the saints. Romans 2:4 Or do you think lightly of the riches of His kindness and tolerance and patience, not knowing that the kindness of God leads you to repentance?

Galatians 5:22-23 But the fruit of the Spirit is love, joy, peace, patience, kindness, goodness, faithfulness, gentleness, self-control; against such things there is no law. Luke 6:35 "But love your enemies, and do good, and lend, expecting nothing in return; and your reward will be great, and you will be sons of the Most High; for He Himself is kind to ungrateful and evil men. Colossians 3:12 So, as those who have been chosen of God, holy and beloved, put on a heart of compassion, kindness, humility, gentleness and patience; Proverbs 3:3 Do not let kindness and truth leave you; Bind them around your neck, Write them on the tablet of your heart.

John 3:16 "For God so loved the world, that He gave His only begotten Son, that whoever believes in Him shall not perish, but have eternal life. Micah 6:8 He has told you, O man, what is good; And what does the LORD require of you But to do justice, to love kindness, And to walk humbly with your God?

Oct 29, 2017, 8:33 AM

I won't tag the person who helped or who was helped for sake of privacy and dignity, but they know who they are. One of my family member's cars broke down yesterday in the freezing weather and a friend "A" was 1 of only 2 people within about 1 1/2 hours time of waiting on roadside assistance who actually stopped to offer help.

Thank you so much "A" for helping my loved one. You have no idea how much that blessed me knowing that you checked upon my loved one. God will not forget your labor of love and, I pray, neither will I. May God's blessings continue to overshadow you. You are a blessing from God.

Mar 7, 2020, 7:35 AM

Why do so many people get jealous of other people doing well and succeeding? Have you ever considered that they are probably SO inspired by YOUR life and YOUR testimonies and may be blessed because of YOUR prayers WHY they are doing so well or are so encouraged? Isn't that what you intended to do?? Isn't that what you prayed for?

Why are you mad? Ain't nobody mad but the devil. Why hate then?! Human nature is so fickle. People hate the good they produce. You planted a whole garden of beautiful flowers and now you want to stop watering it??! That's why so many of our families can't get ahead and suffering because of hate, greed, selfishness and jealousy. God please help us all.

May 15, 2018, 7:11 AM

I saw 2 license plates today within 5 minutes apart. They

read 'YB MEAN' (why be mean) and 'HATE NO MO' (hate no more).

Jun 22, 2018, 11:33 PM

"I used to think that the worst thing in life was to end up alone. It's not. The worst thing in life is to end up with people who make you feel alone." - Robin Williams

Jun 10, 2018, 6:54 AM

A close friend of mine taught me that reaching out to help pull others up, save and encourage someone else even when you feel yourself sinking, helps you to overcome.

Jan 4, 2019, 7:36 AM

You may have thought, "I try to do good for everyone and my efforts are still not appreciated. I feel discouraged. Why do I even bother?"

Word of Encouragement: "And let us not be weary in well doing: for in due season we shall reap, if we faint not." Galatians 6:9

Jul 26, 2019, 8:23 AM

Walk in forgiveness and humility. Don't let the ones who offended you dictate how you respond. Love them anyway even if you have to do it from a distance.

Apr 11, 2020, 10:59 AM

This is my motto all day every day. Love hard. Forgive often and especially if we know we often fall short. I know I fall

short often and even when I try hard not to. And I try to inspire others to always be greater, wiser, stronger and so much
more.

Apr 14, 2019, 9:19 AM

God loves everybody. Love God. Love people. Get right so
you can live right and treat people right. I love you and I'm
rooting for you.

Jul 15, 2020, 9:27 AM

I love you all. I forgive you. If I or my family, my children,
cousins, husband, friends or loved ones have ever offended any
of you or anybody and/or misrepresented our Heavenly Father, please forgive us and please keep us in your prayers that
God's will be done in all our lives and that we will all surrender to His Majesty. Love is what we all need. I need you to survive. I love you

Sincerely,

Your friend, sister, Mom, daughter, Aunt, coworker, associate, business partner, cousin, niece, granddaughter, etc.

Jul 25, 2020, 12:17 PM

I had a wonderful approximate 3- hour conversation with
two beautiful people early this morning at an appointment –
a Mom and her daughter.

They said people normally attack them because of their
beliefs as a Wiccan and an Atheist who identifies as bisexual.
They were in awe that I didn't attack them AND they did not
want to leave my presence because of the love with compassion and genuine concern I had for them along with the words

I was inspired to say to them through God speaking to my thoughts.

Let us not forget how much God loves everybody. Look beyond people's faults to see their needs. Show love first. People don't care how much you know until they know how much you care. Love with compassion. What The World Needs Now Is Love. Love Thy Neighbor.

Jul 17, 2020, 12:29 AM

Evil has a stronghold in your life because of un-forgiveness. ALWAYS ask Jesus to help you forgive and pray for those who offended you.

Aug 23, 2020, 9:32 AM

How can we say we love God and hate our brother or sister?

Sep 4, 2020, 7:44 AM

Forgive. Your eternal life depends upon it.

Aug 30, 2020, 9:56 AM

We all need love, mercy and grace. We shouldn't be too quick to judge and learn to put our pride to the side. Some people are willing to give up on life because so many people have turned their backs on them. Mental health is serious. Show love to people.

Sometimes you never know what a person is struggling with. It can be anxiety, suicidal thoughts, depression, past abuse and so much more. Show love. We all need grace.

Sep 19, 2020, 8:22 AM

How will we handle those who mishandled us?
Oct 9, 2020, 1:44 PM

The disciples of Jesus Christ have love one to another.
Sep 20, 2020, 8:51 AM

By this shall all men know that ye are my disciples, if ye have love one to another.
Oct 13, 2020, 7:27 AM

If you hate your brother or sister in Christ with or without what you see as just cause, then you are a murderer who has committed a heinous crime and tried to hide the evidence. Be sure of this that God is watching from above and your sins (evidence of the murder) will find you out. Turn yourself in. Be convicted by the Holy Spirit.
Oct 18, 2020, 8:27 AM

We all need mercy and God's forgiveness. Sin is sin - lying, stealing, cheating, idol worship, drunkenness, committing physical and spiritual fornication, sowing discord, hatred, bitterness, pride, jealousy, un-forgiveness, etc.
Oct 27, 2020, 11:08 AM

New mercies we see. New mercies we give, right?
Oct 18, 2020, 9:43 AM

"ANGER makes you smaller while FORGIVENESS forces you to grow beyond what you were." - Cherrie Carter-Scott.
Mar 6, 2014, 6:55 AM

Happy Friday! TGIF (Thank God it's Friday) Today I will walk in forgiveness so God can forgive me for my sinful ways (Matthews 6:14). I FORGIVE YOU.
Oct 4, 2013, 10:29 AM

FORGIVENESS - I forgive because I don't want anything stopping my communication with my Father in Heaven ---not even my own unforgiving heart. I FORGIVE YOU.
Oct 4, 2013, 2:19 PM

"To err is human; to forgive, divine." - Alexander Pope
Ask Jesus to help you to forgive.
Nov 15, 2013, 1:04 PM

Dawn Kellum is feeling loved.
I spoke to Jesus last night about ALL the people who have broken my heart because of THEIR broken promises. I said "Jesus, please help me. I don't know what to do." He said, "You are hurt because people didn't uphold their promises. Have you upheld all the promises YOU made to people? YOU are feeling the same hurt that you caused to other people because of YOUR broken promises. If you want me to forgive you of your broken promises, you MUST forgive others who hurt you because of THEIR broken promises to you." I humbly said "Yes. Lord. I forgive. Please help me to forgive."

Nov 21, 2013, 6:46 AM

During the pandemic of 2020, I had the opportunity to care for two very close family members who were suffering with Covid-19. Many people feared contracting the virus. I consulted healthcare professionals for the best methods to boost my immune system (Vitamin D, Vitamin C, Zinc and Multi-Vitamin) and protect myself from contracting Covid-19 (Masks, washing exposed hair and clothing, etc.)

I went and did what was necessary to care for them, i.e., prepare meals, wash clothing, clean, grocery shop, pickup prescription medicine and vitamins, hospital and doctor visit transportation, feeding assistance, consulting healthcare professionals on their behalf, provide temporary housing and so much more.

There are many people suffering and fearful. Do what you can to help others if they want you to help. If not, send others to help them, follow peace with all people and always remember to keep them in your prayers. Romans 15:1 states, "We then that are strong ought to bear the infirmities of the weak, and not to please ourselves."

CHAPTER 14

The Love of a Parent

My daddy and I were talking about that awesome action word "L O V E" this afternoon - even when people hate you, treat you wrong, talk bad about you, etc. I felt SOOO inspired from my Daddy's advice AND I told both my Mom and my Dad, "I love you." They both smiled and said, "I love you too."
Dec 13, 2013, 10:29 PM

Today is March 9. I'm sending a shout-out of Happy Birthday to my son. I gave birth to a bouncing baby boy who was a miracle baby. I almost died having him. He too almost died while I was in labor. His heart rate was well into the 200s and he was in severe fetal distress. The medical team was trying to induce my labor due to our near-fatal complications; however, I was only able to dilate to 2 1/2 cm no matter what they used. 10 cm is required to give birth to a child through the birth canal. The doctors found out late that my birth canal was too narrow to give birth to a child in this manner. I had to have an emergency C-Section. This was all new to me.

My beloved mom, who was very sick at the time and barely

able to see, drove BY HERSELF almost 100 miles to the hospital I was in AT NIGHT AND WALKED IN THE DARK FROM her VERY distant parking space to be with me the ENTIRE time I was in pre-labor and after my son was born. My MOM ALSO held my hand during my EMERGENCY C-SECTION. I was young and scared, but her presence meant so much to me. I will never forget how I kept looking at her asking questions. She would constantly reassure me of what was going on and used comforting words.

I remember upon initial arrival to the hospital, she wouldn't eat or sleep for days, but prayed almost consistently for me and her grandson.

After my son was delivered by emergency C-Section, I was transported to the recovery area for observation, monitoring and surgery recovery. I began shivering uncontrollably. No matter how much cover I had on, I couldn't stop from shivering. I was terrified as this was completely unfamiliar. Suddenly, I heard a familiar voice from outside the curtain, "Dawn! Dawn!" I responded, "Daddy! Daddy! I'm over here." I felt so much more calm, although I couldn't stop the shivering. Once Daddy prayed for me I was fine. Having my Mom and Dad there brought great peace and reassurance.

My 3-year old keeps coming downstairs trying to sneak into the popsicles. The first time she sneaked down the stairs she whispered to herself, "Where she at? Where she at?" as she glided on the floor. I caught her and she ran back up the stairs to bed. Now she is back again looking up at the freezer with a longing look. She doesn't know I'm watching her from my room that offsets the kitchen. She normally doesn't sneak out the bed to get food. She must love those yummy popsicles. Mommy is watching you. I love my children.

Mar 31, 2014, 9:38 PM

Dawn Kellum is feeling thankful.

I am thankful for the best jewelry a Mom could have around her neck - the arms of my children

Nov 14, 2014, 8:02 PM

In 1996, at the approximate age of 20, I worked as a Civil Technology/Engineering Intern for the MDOT (Michigan Department of Transportation) Construction and Technology Division's Bituminous unit. One morning, I was tasked the responsibility of driving a huge, wide and heavy asphalt core truck to a highway construction site approximately 70 miles away from home base to help collect core samples for evaluation, testing and to ensure proper installation of products. I was grateful that, although I had to drive this truck by myself, I was able to follow another coworker in another company truck.

We set out early morning to Grand Rapids, MI while it was still dark. The core truck was only able to go up to about 55-60 miles per hour. I was extremely nervous driving this super slow truck, but I figured that I would eventually catch up to my other co-worker driving and/or he would eventually slow down to wait on me. The other co-worker eventually was nowhere in sight no matter how far I drove.

Suddenly, near Portland, MI, smoke started coming from the truck and it was puttering and making strange noises. Smoke encompassed the cab and the outside of the car. I didn't know what was happening. I was definitely praying. Thankfully, in the midst of speeding semi-trucks and other fast-moving vehicles, I was able to safely pull over to the side of the road.

I had no cell phone or method to communicate to call for help so I knew I had to walk somewhere to get help. I gathered contact information from the glove compartment and put on my high-visibility safety vest. I remembered how my Dad used to walk miles on dark freeways - even in bad weather - to go find help when vehicles broke down on our way to church conferences. My Dad believed that God would take care of him and his family. If my Dad could do it, I could too.

I walked on that dark freeway to the nearest Portland exit for approximately 1 mile. Some people pulled over to ask if I needed I ride, but I didn't trust them so I kept walking. Once I got to the exit there was a store. I walked into the store and was calling to a person standing afar to help me. They appeared to be scared and did not help me whatsoever. I then left there and walked approximately 1 - 2 additional miles down a wooded, country road to a school bus depot. Hallelujah! They helped me. Thank God! I didn't go whimpering back home either. My company sent a gentleman in a flatbed truck, we went back to the location of the broke-down core truck, he placed it on the flatbed truck and drove it back to home base, I got a rental car and drove it ALL the way back to where my team was in the Grand Rapids area. My coworker was in tears apologizing. I forgave him. Hahahaha. I had a big check from that day!

I told my son yesterday after leaving yet another doctor's appointment with yet another $400 prescription, "We don't always pick our journeys in life and know what we will face in life, but wherever life takes us know that ALL things work out together for the good of them that love and know God."

It doesn't FEEL good, but I know that somehow it will work out for our good. I trust that God will take care of us no matter what the situation and no matter what we face. Why should we feel discouraged?

Jul 1, 2014, 9:33 PM

Dawn Kellum was celebrating Gold Star Mother's Day.

Happy Mother's Day to Moms everywhere! Your love for your children and others' children will not go unrewarded.

May 10, 2015, 2:40 AM

Dawn Kellum is feeling thankful.

"God, I thank you that all my children have their five senses and more. God, I thank you for healing my children. God, I thank you for blessing me to have healthy children even AFTER the doctors gave me a bad report."

Nov 21, 2014, 7:46 PM

Happy Mother's Day to you who have been assigned by God to nurture His offspring. May our Father & the keeper of ALL souls continue to give you strength, knowledge of His will and surround you with His loving arms now and forever. Hugs and much love..

May 7, 2016, 6:50 AM

Dawn Kellum was attending Annie at Grand Rapids Civic Theatre.

As my daughters and I watched the live play about orphan Annie last evening, many, including myself, became emotional when Daddy Warbucks showed compassion and love to Annie. I couldn't help but think about our heavenly Father and how nothing can separate us from the love of our "true Father." God loves us and always has our best interest at heart. His son, Jesus Christ, is bringing us back into fellowship with our true Father.

Nov 19, 2017, 5:32 AM

Personally, I've had multiple miscarriages (nearly died with one of them); but, In honor of any parent who has lost a child - asking if everyone will post this as their status for one hour. I'm not sure who will. Think of someone you know or love who has lost their baby or their child. My wish is that we will always take a few minutes to remember these loved ones. Will you post for one hour to honor our Angels? From my personal experience, this is the most painful feeling that never goes away. My prayers and love are with you always!!!

Sep 30, 2017, 2:26 PM

I love the Mothers in the church. They are such an inspiration and a blessing.

Sep 11, 2017, 5:41 AM

...one of my children woke up with a slight nose bleed and I placed a small bag of ice on her neck and prayed for her. She's fine now. It reminds me of the time I used to have multiple nose bleeds as a child and my Dad (RIH) would put his keys in the freezer or into the freezing weather outdoors. After the keys were very cold, he placed them on my neck. I would shake every time those keys touched my neck. Those keys were FREEZIN'! He would then say, "Here you go Dawn. Place that right there..." and then started praying for me. Then the nose bleed would go away. Precious Memories. Oh how they linger!

Jul 18, 2020, 9:07 AM

They are the children God has graciously given your servant.

Genesis 33:5 Honor your father and your mother, so that you may live long in the land the LORD your God is giving you. Exodus 20:12 Impress them on your children. Talk about them when you sit at home and when you walk along the road, when you lie down and when you get up. Deuteronomy 6:7 Keep his decrees and commands, which I am giving you today, so that it may go well with you and your children after you and that you may live long in the land the LORD your God gives you for all time. Deuteronomy 4:40 Through the praise of children and infants you have established a stronghold against your enemies, to silence the foe and the avenger. Psalm 8:2 Children are a heritage from the LORD, offspring a reward from him. Psalm 127:3 Start children off on the way they should go, and even when they are old they will not turn from it. Proverbs 22:6 Folly is bound up in the heart of a child, but the rod of discipline will drive it far away. Proverbs 22:15 Listen, my son, to your father's instruction and do not forsake your mother's teaching. They are a garland to grace your head and a chain to adorn your neck. Proverbs 1:8-9 All your children shall be taught by the LORD, and great shall be the peace of your children. Isaiah 54:13 Children's children are a crown to the aged, and parents are the pride of their children. Proverbs 17:6 They are always generous and lend freely; their children will be a blessing. Psalm 37:26 May the LORD cause you to flourish, both you and your children. Psalm 115:14 Like arrows in the hands of a warrior are children born in one's youth. Psalm 127:4 Whoever spares the rod hates their children, but the one who loves their children is careful to discipline them. Proverbs 13:24

May 4, 2018, 7:10 AM

Happy Mother's Day Mommies. PLEASE REMEMBER TO ALWAYS LISTEN (even while sleeping) TO THAT STILL SMALL VOICE FROM YOUR BABY'S CREATOR. THIS IS THE ONE WHO SPEAKS THROUGH MANY WAYS.

I love you all!

May 12, 2019, 7:47 AM

I have willingly passed up many opportunities to be there

for my children and God always blesses and makes a way. Children come from God and through us. Be a good steward over who God has allowed you to tend and care for.

Sep 10, 2020, 6:51 AM

My GOAL is to teach my children about the one they came FROM and the one they return TO - GOD the FATHER of ALL creation.

Scenario: WHAT IF my husband and I were asked to go overseas for a certain amount of years and we had to entrust our children to another family. I would WANT that other family to TELL my children about us because we PLAN TO COME BACK to get them. THEY CANNOT GO BACK WITH US IF THEY HAVE NOT learned to LOVE and KNOW US even if we are not PHYSICALLY there. How can they not teach MY CHILDREN about US.

How can we be sons and daughters of God and NOT LEARN HOW TO LOVE AND KNOW HIM? Happy Sunday Everyone.

Nov 24, 2013, 7:47 AM

To all the parents out there, remember that children cannot be anything other than children...

Dec 17, 2013, 6:47 PM

Matters of Dignity:

I have learned to not share everything publicly about my children in order to maintain their dignity.

CHAPTER 15

The Gift of Life

I was trying to express what God placed in my Spirit about the gift of every breath AND He told me that someone already wrote what I was trying to express...so He helped me to locate the following quote by THOMAS MERTON:

"To be grateful is to recognize the Love of God in everything He has given us – and He has given us everything. Every breath we draw is a gift of His love, every moment of existence is a grace, for it brings with it immense graces from Him. Gratitude therefore takes nothing for granted, is never unresponsive, is constantly awakening to new wonder and to praise of the goodness of God. For the grateful person knows that God is good, not by hearsay but by experience. And that is what makes all the difference." – Thomas Merton

I almost lost my 2nd born child after 9 confirmed miscarriages (1 near-fatal miscarriage was at 2 months gestation). Around 4 -5 months gestation, I had started to bleed and could no longer feel my 2nd-born child moving. I contacted the doctor and they wanted me to wait it out, drink orange juice, etc. I prayed earnestly for nearly 2 days. I prayed LIFE for my child. Then I went into the bathroom, prayed and asked God, "Is this for naught?" God responded in a still, small voice within my spirit and said, "No. It's not for naught." I then waited about another day and, then, I started to feel my child moving again. She was born healthy at 40 weeks gestation. Hallelujah!

Being a Christian is about serving and recognizing Jesus as the greatest always. He is the sustainer of life and will give you the strength you need.

Jul 12, 2017, 6:41 AM

Dawn Kellum updated her status.

I Praise God for another day. This IS the day that God our creator made. Yesterday is gone. You made it to this day because your life book on earth has more victory pages that MUST be fulfilled. Why? Because GOD wrote it AND because GOD said so - NOT anyone else.

May 22, 2015, 6:17 AM

Matthew 16:24-26 (AMP)

24 Then Jesus said to His disciples, If anyone desires to be My disciple, let him deny himself [disregard, lose sight of, and forget himself and his own interests] and take up his cross and

follow Me [cleave steadfastly to Me, conform wholly to My example in living and, if need be, in dying, also].

25 For whoever is bent on saving his [temporal] life [his comfort and security here] shall lose it [eternal life]; and whoever loses his life [his comfort and security here] for My sake shall find it [life everlasting].

26 For what will it profit a man if he gains the whole world and forfeits his life [his blessed life in the kingdom of God]? Or what would a man give as an exchange for his [blessed] life [in the kingdom of God]?

Apr 13, 2014, 8:15 AM

Dawn Kellum updated her status.

..enjoying these MANY days off - PRICELESS

"remember, life is a precious gift, love is a wonderful gift, and laughter is a glorious gift....So live life to the fullest, love with all your heart, and laugh as much as you breathe." - author unknown

Jun 10, 2014, 8:28 AM

I thank God for allowing me to celebrate another birthday with my husband today and our children had the chance to celebrate their Dad.

May 11, 2015, 9:27 PM

I realize that my existence and my awareness of my existence is a miracle.

Nov 16, 2014, 2:43 AM

Dawn Kellum was in United States.
Place: United States
New day. New victories. Thank God for another day.
Oct 13, 2015, 6:52 AM

Although I was sad to have missed church last Sunday due to multiple deadly contagious illnesses I contracted because of a suppressed immune system, MY friend was kind enough to text me the following sermon snippet from our church.

The message today was "You Matter"

The text was Psalm 139:1-14. Verse 14: You are fearfully and wonderfully made. It was a good message to remind us that we all matter to God. He knows the number of hairs on our head. He knows and understands everything we go through - and He cares. He loves us so much that He sent His son to die for us. We even matter to Jesus so much so that He hung there on the cross and endured the pain. We matter to God. Good word!"

Jul 1, 2016, 6:30 AM

I woke up this morning to my husband frantically trying to find a heartbeat on different parts of my chest and neck. He could not find a heartbeat AT ALL. He asked me "Are you alive?" I looked at him like he was crazy and said, "Of course."

STORY MORAL - Certainly, we live, move, and exist because of Him

(God). As some of your poets have said, 'We are God's children.' Ref. Acts 17:28

Dec 7, 2013, 11:28 AM

Thank you God for giving me a NEW day I've NEVER seen before & SO much more. Don't take God's blessings for granted. God took time & effort to allow you to HAVE the blessings. Take time & effort to appreciate them. That's how God KNOWS that you're thankful.

Dec 19, 2013, 6:42 AM

...that time in our lives where we must completely depend upon God for everything including our next breath. Pray.

Mar 18, 2020, 6:12 AM

We get one life to live on this earth. We should never look down upon or treat others wrong, because, as the world turns, so may the tables. We reap what we sow not just for one season; but, possibly throughout the days of our lives and for all of our children.

Nov 30, 2018, 6:59 PM

As a volunteer for patients in hospice care, the gift of presence (being there) is one of the greatest gifts. It is heartbreaking to walk into a facility and see many faces turn to you expecting their loved ones - only to be disappointed and turn their heads back in sadness. The family pictures, memoirs, a stranger's help, money and other gifts left with them cannot replace a familiar voice or a familiar presence.

Recognize also that some with dementia feel "lost" and cannot recognize objects like telephones, food, etc. They are almost like little babies in regards to cognitive abilities.

They should be respected with the utmost respect and re-member to always maintain their dignity even when they may have forgotten how.

Feb 1, 2020, 8:52 AM

Life in these earthly bodies is like a vapor. We don't know when we will leave them. My manager's husband passed away suddenly. He was preparing to retire. I pray for her and her family's continued strength as well as so many of us who are grieving loved ones who have passed on.

Jan 30, 2020, 2:01 PM

CHAPTER 16

God of Comfort, Please Comfort Me

RIP (Rejoice in Paradise) to my Mom who passed away January 19, 2014. Will the Circle be Unbroken? This song refers to the family circle - Mother, Dad, sisters and brothers - knowing all would pass some day. I remember that my Mother's faith in Jesus created strong faith in my whole family. I know mother has gone to her Heavenly reward to be with Jesus Christ forever.

I wonder if my whole family will keep the faith she taught us. When we all pass away one day, will we all die with our Faith in Jesus Christ? Will our entire family circle be reunited with our Mother in heaven or will any of my family lose their faith because Mom's physical presence is no longer here to guide us to keep faith in Jesus Christ? Will any of us be left out when we all meet again? Will we find AND keep our own relationship with Christ Jesus since He is the ONLY way to eternal life. Will we all, one day, be reunited in Heaven with my Mom or will some of us lose our way?

Try Jesus for Yourself: The Day my Mom Died

Sunday Morning, January 19, 2014 – I still remember this day as if it were yesterday. I got myself and my two little girls ready for church. I was careful to make sure we all had on our Sunday Best outfits, church shoes/boots and that our hair was decent. We ate a scrumptious breakfast that morning. My husband and I try to make sure our breakfasts are scrumptious before church every Sunday. It is rare for us to have "cereal-only" breakfasts on Sunday. The breakfast meals normally consist of grits, cheese toast, butter biscuits, turkey sausage and cheese eggs with various types of juices and/or water. The weather was quite cold that day. It was indeed a cold, bitter day in January. There was a high of 29 degrees and a low of 11 degrees. Although the weather was quite bitter, I was still in a joyful mood and elated to be going to church to hear the anointed praises of God and the word of God.

Once we got to church, I brought my two little girls to the children's church where children are taught the word of God in a format that is fitting for their age. I then proceeded to the main sanctuary with a joyful heart of worship to God. I remember one of the psalmists sung the song "Total Praise" by Richard Smallwood. Some of the lyrics are as follows:

Lord, I will lift my eyes to the hills
Knowing my help is coming from You
Your peace You give me in time of the storm

You are the source of my strength
You are the strength of my life
I lift my hands in total praise to You

RHEMA WORD

The sermon preached during Sunday's service was "Try Him for Yourself". Excerpts from the message are as follows:

We must have an individual relationship with Jesus Christ. Jesus is the source of everything we need. Psalms 34:8 – "O taste and See" - St. John 6:24-36-37. You can't taste God if you don't trust Him. Before you taste of God, you must believe that He exists. Our whole existence is to glorify God. The only thing that stood between the Israelites and the Promised Land was the condition of their heart.

God don't owe us anything; but, we owe God everything. One must believe that God is real. Believe that God is our hope. Jesus Christ is the answer to the human condition. God's motives are pure. You have got to experience God for yourself. Remember the Woman at the well? God is deeper than the well. Remember how Jesus fed the 5000. Only God can do the impossible. Jesus blessed the loaves. Jesus is the savior of the whole world. Jesus will make you whole and take you from earth to glory. He will blow your mind. Remember when Jesus walked on water. He controls the elements. You can't give your life to Jesus just for the goodies. St. John 6:26. Elevate your mind to the spiritual. St. John 6:27. Don't pull all your energy into the things that don't last until everlasting life. It's important to have a relationship with Jesus. You don't always need rules and being under control freaks. Jesus Christ is the permanent fix to an eternal condition. Your soul will never be spiritually hungry or thirsty. O taste and see that the Lord is good. Jesus Christ is the source of all of our needs. Tell the ones already born again, "I will not let anyone pluck you out of my hand. I am the source of all your needs. Hold on to me.

AFTER THE SERMON

Once this RHEMA WORD from Heaven was spoken, the Pastor asked people to come forward to the altar that wanted to get stronger spiritually. I chose to stay at my seat and pray. During this time I felt my telephone vibrating uncontrollably inside my purse. There was an overabundance of text messages on my telephone. I knew something was wrong.

Then my cousin called me on the telephone crying with great concern "Dawn, your MOM passed." I tried to keep my composure and responded "What? My Mom passed?!?!"

She proceeded to tell me that my family was at the hospital where they had pronounced her dead and to meet my family there. She also let me know that my husband and son were on their way to help drive me to the hospital. I gathered all my belongings and stood up and gave a message to the ushers to let my Pastor know that my Mom had passed and immediately walked out to go get my daughters from the children's church.

I barely made it up the stairs before I broke down and starting sobbing on my way to the children's church. I felt SO weak from grief. I was fighting hard to keep it together until I could feel an unexplainable peace come over me. I then had the strength to go to the children's church to pickup my daughters. I informed the teacher present that my Mom had just passed. She expressed her condolences and gave me a hug. I then told my daughters. They became sad. Upon leaving the children's church, I went to the bathroom.

I proceeded to call one of my sister-in-law's to tell her of the news on my mother's passing. Once I called her, I said, "I just wanted to let you know that my Mom passed." She then proceeded to say, "How are you doing?" Once she said that I shrieked into nearly uncontrollable tears. She was very supportive and offered words of comfort to calm me down. I thank God for her answering the telephone and being a listening ear. Once I was finally able to calm down, I gathered my belongings and proceeded out of the bathroom to the church vestibule where some of the church mothers were selling cakes. I reached in my purse to pay for the cakes until one of the mothers stopped me and said, "No. You don't need to pay. Just take what you want." I thanked her and proceeded towards the door.

I then saw my husband and son coming to accompany me to the hospital to be with my family. As I followed my husband and son to the hospital, I tried not to think too much about my mother's passing.

That was one of the toughest days of my life; however, I somehow knew that God was still with me through it all giving me comfort and grace to stand.

My Mom went to Paradise AKA HEAVEN to be with Jesus that day Sunday, January 19, 2014 at the age of 75. She fought the good fight, finished the race AND kept the faith unto death. Now is laid up for her a crown of RIGHTEOUSNESS (Reference 2 Timothy 4:7-8).

For her to live is Christ – Whether she lives or dies, Christ was gain to her. While she lived she was Christ's property and servant, and Christ is HER portion; if she dies – if she be called to witness the truth at the expense of her life or if she dies keeping the faith in Jesus Christ, this will be gain; she shall be saved from the remaining troubles and difficulties in life and be placed immediately and PERMANENTLY in possession of HER heavenly inheritance. As, therefore, it respects herself, it is a matter of perfect indifference to her whether she be taken off by sudden death, or whether she be permitted to continue here on earth any longer; in either case she LOSES NOTHING. (Reference Philippians 1:21).

INSPIRED

I thank GOD for the RHEMA WORD I received from heaven a few minutes prior to me finding out about my Mom's sudden death through my Pastor to "Try Jesus for yourself."

I could no longer depend upon Mom's prayers any more. I could no longer depend upon Mom's faith for the things that I desired. It was time for me to gain a closer relationship to God because the good that my Mom imparted to me and SO many others was because of God's grace. It was time for me to try Jesus Christ for myself in a deeper relationship... I have to know Jesus Christ for myself.

May the grace of our Lord Jesus Christ, and the love of God, and the fellowship of the Holy Spirit be with us all, now and evermore.

God's Comfort through a Heavenly Song

November 5, 2013 – I was up most of the night/morning meditating on God's word and thinking about loved ones passed on. I knew I had to go into work in the morning so I proceeded to read a scripture, say a prayer and fell asleep. I had the following dream/vision/not completely certain:

I was shown a lot of things about a lot of people still here on earth. Then I went to another place where people who had died serving Christ Jesus were enjoying themselves praising God, etc. They were STILL ALIVE!!! I remember seeing my dear Aunt who passed on some time ago. She was sharp and her face was flawless. She was very calm. I sat down next to her. She took my hand and we BOTH started singing a song that I've NEVER heard before called "HOLY, HOLY, HOLY, HOLY." It was the most beautiful song I ever heard.

Then people started telling me to stop singing and let go...but I didn't want to stop singing because I could feel the presence of God; His peace; His love, etc. and **I did NOT want ANYTHING OR ANYBODY else other than THIS PRESENCE; THIS PEACE; THIS LOVE, ETC.**

Then I passed through many "clouds" and woke up with SO MUCH PEACE and could STILL hear the angels singing HOLY. The peace of God surpasses ALL understanding and comforts our hearts and minds. Jesus Christ is here with us. We are NOT alone.

What about those who die in Christ? If we die as a Christian, we STILL live in Christ - just not of this world; but He takes us into a place called Paradise until Jesus Christ comes back and we rise in the "rapture" to continue to spend eternity with him forever. He that liveth and believeth in Christ Jesus shall never die. When believers in Christ Jesus who love and know Him are absent from the body, they are present with the Lord. In a recent vision, the Lord showed me that earthly bodies cannot contain the level of glory applied to those who have passed on. They are exposed to a weightier level of glory.

KNOW that Jesus Christ is the ONLY one who has the keys to death, hell and the grave. He has power over death. Those who "pass away" in Christ Jesus are currently in paradise – which from many people's testimonies who have died and came back to life to this world, incl. my sister-in-law, speak highly of its beauty and how it is a glorified and enhanced version of earth – where there is a sun brighter than earth's sun, where your skin is refreshed and anew, where the grass is freshly green, where there are colors you have never seen on earth. Many colors in Paradise are mentally incomprehensible down here on earth where your human brain cannot comprehend them. There is so much more there to see. A brother of mine had a vision of my sister showing her mansion to him. Afar you can also see hell's torment and the smoke coming up from it. Christians who have passed on are enjoying themselves in paradise until Jesus Christ comes back in what is called "the Rapture" [Ref. I Corinthians 15:51] and raises them back up from Paradise with new and more glorified bodies to be with Him forever and partake in ALL that he has prepared.

In the rapture, we who are still alive on this earth will

ALSO be gathered together with the "dead in Christ" to meet the Lord Jesus Christ in the air and so shall we EVER be with the Lord. We don't have to sorrow as others who have no hope because we can place hope in Jesus Christ.

..through grief and loss, I am a witness that God is the comforter. God has plans already in action to help you through any loss or grief. Be encouraged dear hearts.

May 15, 2015, 7:18 PM

II Corinthians 5:1 [AMP]

For we know that if the tent which is our earthly home is destroyed (dissolved), we have from God a building, a house not made with hands, eternal in the heavens.

Aug 22, 2014, 9:30 PM

"Can you still believe in Me when your life's a living hell? And when all the things around you seem to quickly fade away?

I know how bad it hurt you when that loved one's life came to an end

And when they had to leave you, you said you'd NEVER love again

But will you trust that I can help you and I'll never turn

away? Will you trust Me, child, no matter, come what may?"
- Donnie Mcclurkin - "I'll Trust You"

Aug 26, 2014, 6:15 AM

When you trust God to bring comfort, He will do it where you KNOW it's from Him and you continue to lean on Him

Oct 10, 2020, 6:05 AM

Dawn Kellum is feeling heartbroken.

RIP "Sweety" Kellum. We're going to miss our baby - gone too soon. We will be heading to the park shortly for her proper burial. Since we loved "Sweety", will she be in our mansion on high? Although I haven't had a personal revelation of this or read this in scripture, but I somehow believe our beloved pets will be in the hereafter with us after this life is over. We miss our guinea pig.

Jun 9, 2015, 5:58 PM

My Pastor Bishop Dr. Alfred Singleton Sr has passed away and gone from labor to reward. My prayers go out to my Singleton and Breadhouse church family and loved ones for continued comfort, strength and more as we grieve this great man of God who was compassionate, divinely anointed and appointed, loving, a man of integrity and great morale, filled with the Holy Spirit, a man after God's own heart, one of great wisdom and knowledge, a pastor at heart, in truth and in deeds.

"Our hearts are broken in many pieces; but, we, as fellow

believers of Christ Jesus, will see you in God's tomorrow. Thank you also for all the times you stopped by our house as kids to bless our family with gifts and more. My Dad spoke highly of you and how you have been a great help to many since he moved to Lansing over 40 years ago. You had the heart of God and loved people. You are missed and never forgotten."

A few days before my Pastor passed away, I had a vision of him. He was sitting on what appeared to be a park-like bench under what appeared to be a small park shelter. He had what appeared to be some type of basket on the ground in front of him. He sat there feverishly sweating profusely while working super hard on many "contents" in the basket. I felt immediate compassion and wanted to help him and reach to help him and wanting him to slow down – but he kept responding to me by saying, "READ. READ. READ." Once I awakened, I received the revelation that his love and compassion for souls was far above what many of us could ever comprehend in this life. He truly gave his life for people and for the Kingdom's sake.

I enjoyed hearing my Pastor sing and I enjoyed the privilege of accompanying him on the keyboard on several occasions. I love to hear him sing, "One Day at a Time." Another one of my favorite songs I loved to hear him sing was called, "God's Tomorrow." The lyrics are as follows:

God's tomorrow is a day of gladness
And its joys shall never fade
No more weeping, no more sense of sadness
No more foes to make afraid

God's tomorrow, God's tomorrow
Every cloud will pass away
At the dawning of that day
God's tomorrow, no more sorrow
For I know that God's tomorrow
Will be better than today

God's tomorrows is a day of greeting
We shall see the Savior's face
And our longing hearts await the meeting
In that holy, happy place

God's tomorrow is a day of glory
We shall wear the crown of life
Sing thro' countless years love's old, old story
Free for ever from all strife
Dec 6, 2017, 5:19 AM

RIH to my Pastor Bishop Singleton. You have fought a good fight and finished your course. You were a man of great wisdom, divine anointing, compassion, integrity, wonderfully talented, inspiring, a giver and so much more. You sacrificed so much for people and your love was genuine and heart-felt. I also thank God for the prophetic vision I had of you a few weeks ago. I will take heed. I'll see you in God's tomorrow. I am yet praying for my Singleton family and my Breadhouse family and all our loved ones as we grieve this great warrior and true man of God.
Dec 6, 2017, 4:39 AM

There is hope beyond the grave.
Aug 8, 2020, 10:47 AM

My Daddy passed away May 7, 2020
My Big Sister passed away May 20, 2020
Where do broken hearts go?
May 21, 2020, 8:29 AM

The same creator who created us knows how to comfort us. The Lord knoweth how!
May 19, 2020, 8:18 AM

Meditating: When your loved ones are no longer able to take care of themselves and/or able to make decisions regarding their health so God takes them so He will take care of them.
Jun 2, 2020, 1:39 PM

May 31, 2020 counseling to me from "Mama Esther" - You don't have to prove anything to anybody that you're grieving. Do only those things that make you happy. Do not respond to people who want you to relive the grief all over again, i.e., what happened, etc. Your body is crying inside. Those are nerves and if you don't stop it can get into your brain so deep and will cause a nervous breakdown. Then you will have to be hospitalized in an institution and, once you have a nervous breakdown, it is hard to come back from one. Stop crying. Your Dad and your sister are fine. They are with Jesus. They are okay. They would not want you crying. Speak in tongues and spend time in worship.

Jun 4, 2020, 7:08 PM

...seeing my sister who passed away in a vision rejoicing and praising God as I glorified God with her was something we often did together before her passing. Those dreams bring great comfort. Thank you heavenly Father for bringing me comfort.

Jul 3, 2020, 7:18 AM

To Family Life Radio:

Good Morning. My name is Dawn. I have been a Christian for many years. My Mom passed away January 19, 2014. After she passed, I felt like I was having a nervous breakdown and wanted to give up. The pain of losing my beloved Mom was too much to bear mentally and emotionally.

I was on my way to work one day and turned on Family Life Radio as I often do. You played the song "Your Grace Finds Me" by Matt Redman. I felt the presence of God's grace surround me at an entirely new level, and, even, in spite of the massive grief I'd been experiencing, I felt so inspired listening to this song. It has helped to bring light to a very dark place in my life. Please continue to pray for me as I go through this very rough journey. God Bless You Family Life Radio

Feb 6, 2014, 11:09 AM

Thank you God for allowing me to see the light at the end of a very dark place I went to after losing my Mom. I am standing on the promises of God and letting Him carry me through. I think I can make it now.

Feb 7, 2014, 7:50 AM

Good Morning FBF (Facebook family). I would like you all to know that God has truly given me GREAT comfort through the passing of many loved ones over the last few months, including, but NOT limited to, many cousins, my Mom, my godmother/spiritual grandmother & my sister-in-law and SO many great women and men of God.

I have also had multiple heavenly visions and much, much more and my Mom is so strong now and beautiful and mentally quick and she comes to me in visions preaching the word of God and encouraging me to do more for God AND that she is waiting on that concert and SO MUCH MORE. God has allowed me to see and experience SO MUCH.

Feb 11, 2014, 6:28 AM

I am thinking about loved ones passed on and those of us still here to war as Christian soldiers. It will all be worth It when we get to Heaven.

Oct 23, 2013, 7:03 PM

Heaven is home. This world is not our permanent home. It's just temporary.

II Cor. 4:18 - What is seen is temporary. What is not seen is eternal. Which of us are going to make it back home to heaven? Unfortunately, all of us won't make it back home. Some will lose their way and choose to remain lost by getting entangled with the yoke of bondage or sin in this present world instead of doing what Jesus Christ told them to do to make it back home. We are here temporarily on this earth to spoil principalities and to make God's praises glorious amongst SO many other things and then go back home. Do YOU KNOW WHO YOU ARE and WHY YOU ARE HERE?

May 18, 2013, 12:24 AM

Questions: SCENARIO. Let's just say FOR EXAMPLE - WHAT if we were ALREADY in Heaven and God said "I am going to place you on earth to fight the devil and spoil principalities and, through it all, make my praises glorious, AND, if you do what I say, you will go to A HIGHER Level in Heaven. HOW WOULD YOU LIVE YOUR LIFE NOW? Remember, this is just a scenario.

May 21, 2013, 2:02 AM

Questions. Questions. Why are people afraid of going up in the rapture when Jesus Christ comes back? We are used to this earth that God has placed us on. Do you think that Heaven will be foreign to you? NO. Heaven is our HOME. When you go home you feel comfortable so do what Jesus Christ said to do and let's go home. ref. I Cor. 2:9

May 21, 2013, 1:53 AM

God has a LOT of good things in store for those who know & love Him - stuff we have NEVER even heard of EVEN throughout eternity. Can you imagine?

Sep 2, 2013, 10:20 AM

Yesterday evening, I was praying for those of us grieving for loved ones gone before. Jesus Christ encouraged my spirit and let me know that we have family (part of the cloud of witnesses) gone before us in Heaven's "grandstands" cheering us on in this race to endure to the end! Ref. Heb. 12:1 Be encouraged. We are not alone in this walk. I believe many, including, but not limited to, my 9 children lost through miscarriage are rooting me on. A WHOLE BUNCH of other loved ones who have gone before us are rooting us on to MAKE it to the end. Let us run this race with patience. "For this cause I bow my knees unto the Father of our Lord Jesus Christ, of whom the whole family in heaven and earth is named." Ref. Ephesians 3:14 and 15

May 11, 2013, 9:17 AM

My heart is heavy. My sister-in-law and my spiritual grandmother Sara Harrison both passed away this weekend. They were true warriors in the kingdom. God said it was time for them to go home. They fought a good fight, finished their course and kept the faith. They are absent from their bodies but present with our Father in Heaven.

Oct 15, 2013, 12:31 AM

Channel 10 News interviewed my brother and our family

yesterday after we all finished the Making Strides against Breast Cancer Walk (3.1 miles) to raise breast cancer awareness & help find a cure for the disease that my brother's wife succumbed to leaving 9 children and 3 step-children and a husband of 10 years. This was a very emotional day.

Oct 27, 2013, 8:40 AM

Rest In Paradise Pastor Brenda Waller. I thank God for your life, testimonies, inspiration, teachings and MORE to ME and SO Many others. You fought the GOOD fight! I will never forget how beautiful of a person you were to me and others.

Nov 1, 2013, 4:22 PM

The ones who care about us are not always gonna' be here on this earth. Treasure them now.

Nov 5, 2013, 2:34 AM

My beloved Sister-in-Law passed away October 12, 2013. Months before she passed away, I sought the Lord for a way to encourage her. I would occasionally sing to her at her bedside, help lift her up physically and otherwise, do her hair, pray with her, offer loving words of encouragement, help out in her home, help out with her babies, speak words of comfort to my brother and more. I loved her dearly. We shared the love of true sisters. She was dearly beloved.

I also wrote a song for her called "Tomorrow" to help encourage her. It is based off of her personality, our meaningful conversations and her perception. The lyrics are as follows.

I don't know what tomorrow may bring but I have a joyful
song to sing

If I never see another moon in June

If I never see another blue-jay in May

If I never feel the touch of a north wind blow again

If I never smell another red rose in the springtime

Hallelujah, Hallelujah. Hallelujah.

If I never see the leaves dance again in the fall-time

If I never see the snow fall anymore in the winter-time

If I never see another sunrise across the ocean

If I never feel the rain again on my brow in the heat of the
day

Hallelujah, Hallelujah. Hallelujah.

I don't know what tomorrow may bring

but I have a joyful song to sing

Bless the Lord at all times.

Matters of Grief: Keep Walking

October 6, 2013 – My beloved and dear cousin departed
this life today.

October 12, 2013 – My beloved godmother departed this
life.

October 14, 2013 My beloved sister-in-law, a mother of 9
children and 3 step children, succumbed to a grave illness.

January 19, 2014 My beloved Mother passed away.

April 2014 My dear friend succumbed to a grave illness.

July 2014 A dear friend of mine – my godmother's daughter – passed away.

July 2014 – My dear friend's beloved son passed away.

August 15, 2014 – A dear friend of mine died suddenly.

These are just a few of the many people who have recently passed away. The list has grown substantially since August. I am deeply saddened; however, I am thankful to God for the lives of these loved ones. It is because of God's grace that I had the opportunity to spend time with them. It was also God's grace that allowed them to be a part of my life. I believe that God is now taking very good care of them because to be absent from the body is to be present with God - although this human body goes back to the dust.

I am comforted in knowing that they all accepted Christ Jesus as their Lord and Savior. They all were baptized in the name of Jesus Christ and received the anointing gift of the Holy Spirit. Upon receiving salvation in Jesus Christ, they led exemplary lives. They were examples of righteousness. They were faithful to God. They loved Jesus Christ and served Him with all their hearts even when they weren't feeling well and didn't feel like it. They loved the people of God. They were all blessed to be parents with beautiful and handsome children that God allowed them to care for. They served God with all their hearts, minds, souls and strength even through sickness, exhaustion, illness and much more.

They are champions. They are victors through Christ Jesus. They are overcomers. They overcame by the blood of the lamb -the son of God crucified at the cross, the word of the testimonies of other believers and they loved Jesus even while they were going through illness and even unto death. This is because they knew that, if this earthly dwelling were to be dissolved, they had another building not made with hands and eternal in the heavens.

I can hardly wait to see them and SO many others again in the hereafter; however, not too soon. My life story is still in process of being written. I believe that I must finish the plan that God has for me to do on earth. I must continue to fight the GOOD fight of faith and lay hold onto the eternal life that is only through Christ Jesus and don't forsake the eternal life that is only through Christ Jesus. I must continue to live for God until my life book on earth is closed.

RHEMA WORD

The following anointed RHEMA WORD gave me further instructions on what I should do now that many of those close to me have gone to be completely in the presence of God. The RHEMA WORD was delivered by way of an illustrated sermon entitled "Quest for a Better and Enduring Substance" preached by my Pastor Sunday, August 17, 2014. August 17, 2014 was also 2 days after a dear friend of mine, who was also a faithful member of our church, passed away suddenly.

DATE: 8.17.14
BIBLICAL TEXT: Hebrews 10:34-35 and Luke 22:31-32
Hebrews 10:34-35
...knowing in yourselves that ye have in heaven a better and an enduring substance. Cast not away therefore your confidence, which hath great recompense of reward.

Luke 22:31-32

...behold, Satan hath desired to have you, that he may sift you as wheat. But I have prayed for thee, that thy faith fail not: and when thou art converted, strengthen thy brethren.

LET THY FAITH FAIL NOT

Let thy Faith fail not. Quest for a better and enduring substance. Quest for the things that are better. Some people are satisfied with the temporal things. Don't cast away your confidence. There is something better and more enduring - Better than this temporary stuff and something that is everlasting. Confidence that drops causes problems. When your confidence is challenged, it becomes a problem. Cast not away therefore your confidence even while in a faith crisis.

What if God said "If I remove all your support system...will you still keep the faith?"

IN THE CRISIS

The devil tries to make you think that God is NOT in the midst of crisis; however, God is deep and masterful. In the crisis, all you see is the pain; but you must know that the end result is going to be for the better because ALL things work out together for the good of them that love the Lord and to them that are called according to His purpose. In the crisis, praise Him. Shake yourself. Come to yourself. Because you have a faith crisis doesn't mean you have no faith. Luke 22:31 – Losing confidence can make you lose focus.

Know that God still cares for us even in crisis. Don't drift away from God listening to the devil. Know that the devil is a liar and the father of them. Even in the crisis, God said He will give you a glimpse of something and let you come up for air every now and then. God will give victory and joy through it all. Give God a praise.

FAITH DON'T FAIL ME NOW

Keep confidence in Jesus. The devil wants to fill you with his garbage. Come what may! Know that Jesus Christ has prayed for us that our faith fail not. Ref. Luke 12:32 Faith don't fail me now. Whatever you're going through, keep pursuing, keep pressing and keep walking. Eventually we're going to make it to our heavenly home.

KEEP WALKING

Know that the will and plan of God is bigger than what you can see.

You've got to keep moving. Keep walking and put on the whole armor of God.

KEEP ON WALKING

I was truly inspired after hearing this RHEMA WORD from God. This was an ON-TIME word from God specifically for what I was going through.

I miss my dearly departed loved ones greatly. I am still grieving; however, I can feel the comfort of God in and around me and I will KEEP WALKING. I will KEEP WALKING on the Quest for a Better and Enduring Substance. I will continue to live for God until I walk from life on earth into life eternity and completely in the presence of God in Heaven.

I must keep walking for God because I know my walking is NOT in vain! Can two walk together, except they be agreed?

(Ref. Amos 3:3) I am walking with God because I agree with His will for my life. I will walk by faith and not just by what I see. I must stay close to the one who loves me the most and the same one who has eternal plans of un-ended blessedness for me, my dearly departed loved ones and ALL other believers. Even though I walk through the valley of the shadow of death, I fear no evil because God's rod and staff comfort me. (Ref. Psalms 23).

If I walk in the Light as He Himself is in the Light, we have fellowship with one another, and the blood of Jesus His Son cleanses us from all sin. But if we walk in the light, as He is in the light, we have fellowship one with another, and the blood of Jesus Christ his Son cleanseth us from all sin. (Reference I John 1:7) I will walk in the manner worthy of the calling with which I have been called. (Reference Eph 4:1)

I will walk in a manner worthy of the Lord, to please God in all respects, bearing fruit in every good work and increasing in the knowledge of God. (Ref. Colossians 1:10)

CONCLUSION

When you feel like giving up or throwing in the towel, KEEP the FAITH. Call out to Jesus Christ. He will give you the strength you need. Keep your faith and confidence in Him. The Lord is close to the broken-hearted. He is with you now. Let Jesus Christ be Lord of your life. Faith in Jesus Christ is faith worth HAVING because ONLY HE has the BETTER AND ENDURING SUBSTANCE.

May the grace of our Lord Jesus Christ, and the love of God, and the fellowship of the Holy Spirit be with you all, now and evermore.

October 27, 2014

CHAPTER 17

Seeing Paradise aka Heaven

Revelation 2:7 Whoever has ears, let them hear what the Spirit says to the churches. To the one who is victorious, I will give the right to eat from the tree of life, which is in the paradise of God.

2 Corinthians 12:2-4 I know a man in Christ who fourteen years ago was caught up to the third heaven. Whether it was in the body or out of the body I do not know - God knows. And I know that this man - whether in the body or apart from the body I do not know, but God knows. was caught up to paradise and heard inexpressible things, things that no one is permitted to tell.

Luke 23:42-43 Then he said, "Jesus, remember me when you come into your kingdom." Jesus answered him, "Truly I tell you, today you will be with me in paradise."

Luke 16:26 And beside all this, between us and you there

is a great gulf fixed: so that they which would pass from hence to you cannot; neither can they pass to us, that would come from thence.

My Sister's Testimony of Paradise

I want to tell you about the Lord bringing me back from the dead. I was in the hospital having twin babies. The word of the Lord says, (Psalms 127:3) "Lo, children are a heritage of the Lord and the fruit of the womb is His reward." My baby girl came out first but the boy didn't come out until two hours or so later. My husband, a Minister, was in the room with me and he said my eyes rolled back in my head and I went out of here. My husband called our Pastor and said I had stopped breathing. My Pastor made it to the hospital in about five minutes. They said there were over 30 doctors in the room trying to resuscitate me. It looked hopeless. My Pastor and my husband laid hands on me and prayed the prayer of faith.

I had died and went to Paradise. I went to a beautiful place where the grass was so green. On this earth there is no comparison to that place. At the end of the grass there was a gulf. When I looked over at the gulf it looked like smoke but it wasn't regular smoke. It was like thick dark clouds going up. There was no fear of that gulf. The ones over there couldn't come where I was and I couldn't go over there. There is no fear or pain in dying.

When I looked at myself I was young again. I had made it to Paradise! Then I heard what sounded like my Pastor calling my name and I went to see what he wanted and came back to this life. My twin babies were born healthy. I am a living witness of God's divine Power and I know God's word is true. Whether we live here or die, we have everything to gain and nothing to lose.

Submitted by my Sister in Christ
Minor Edits by Women Unspotted

My heavenly Father allowed me to visit Paradise aka Heaven at least two times. Here is what I remember about my real HOME.

The City: It was the most beautiful place I had ever seen. I remember seeing the beautiful city with a beautiful garden-like path of extreme beauty. I have seen maybe one picture on the Internet that somewhat depicts it.

The Colors: The colors there were so beautiful and vibrant that, once I came back to my earthly mind and body, my earthly mind could not mentally conceive the colors. One of the colors that stood out the most was a greenish-type color that is NOT here on earth. When I was there I could mentally conceive all the colors; but, my brain in my fleshly body could not conceive them. That was quite frustrating returning to a very limited brain.

The Water and Waterfall: I remember seeing a crystal-like stream that moves. I also saw a purple-like tall sparkling water-fall that sort of swayed.

The People: The people there are so kind and loving. They embrace you, welcome you and are so happy to see you.

The Feeling: You feel immediate love as if you are really HOME and where you belong.

The Unexplained Eternal State: There is still one thing I

cannot explain though. When I visited Paradise aka Heaven, it was like I had ALWAYS been there and had NEVER been here on earth. My return to earth from Paradise is when I realized I had lived somewhere else other than Paradise.

Returning Home: I think about Paradise aka Heaven every day. I believe Jesus Christ wanted me to catch a glimpse and to share my experiences. Once my purpose is fulfilled on this earth, I plan to go back home. There is so much I don't understand beyond this life, but my experience was REAL.

Forever-living vs Forever-dying: This earthly body is temporary, but where will your soul live if you leave your earthly dwelling or human body? While you exist in your earthly body, let Jesus Christ be Lord of your life. Jesus is the way to eternal life. Rejecting Jesus Christ is the way to eternal death or forever dying. Receiving salvation through Jesus Christ alone is the way to eternal life or forever living.

Oct 29, 2020, 7:53 AM

1 Corinthians 2:9 (Amplified Bible) ...but just as it is written [in Scripture], "THINGS WHICH THE EYE HAS NOT SEEN AND THE EAR HAS NOT HEARD, AND WHICH HAVE NOT ENTERED THE HEART OF MAN, ALL THAT GOD HAS PREPARED FOR THOSE WHO LOVE HIM [who hold Him in affectionate reverence, who obey Him, and who gratefully recognize the benefits that He has bestowed]."

I just wanna make it to Heaven. I wanna see my Mom again, my sisters again, my godmother again, my babies lost through miscarriage and the one I regretfully aborted a long time ago. I want to see all my loved ones in Heaven. I just wanna make it to Heaven. I've got to make it to Heaven. I've GOT to see them again. I can't miss Heaven. I've got to make it.

Oct 3, 2016, 10:14 PM

Heaven, heaven
Everybody's talking 'bout heav'n aint going there
Oh heaven
Everybody's talking 'bout heav'n aint going there - Mahalia Jackson - "Walk Over God's Heaven"

Nov 28, 2016, 12:49 PM

And as it is appointed unto men once to die, but after this the judgment:

Mar 14, 2020, 8:12 AM

All earthly bodies will eventually dissolve. This flesh is just temporary. Being born again, not of corruptible seed, but of incorruptible, by the word of God, which liveth and abideth for ever. For all flesh is as grass, and all the glory of man as the flower of grass. The grass withereth, and the flower thereof falleth away: But the word of the Lord endureth for ever. And this is the word which by the gospel is preached unto you.

Aug 22, 2020, 7:03 AM

CHAPTER 18

The Peculiar

The funniest weekly statement thus far by someone I work with is as follows:

"That person that wanted the spotlight is no longer dancing on the stage they thought they created. They are dancing in dirty sand on a beach by themselves." Humble thyself.

Apr 11, 2018, 7:19 PM

Some people are only attracted to each other because their demons know each other - posted by a fellow Christian

May 27, 2015, 9:36 PM

I sung one of my Mom's favorite songs "IN THE MORN-ING WHEN I RISE" at her graveside as other family stood some distance away. My eldest, who has a gift to see in the spiritual realm, saw my Mom standing right there next to me for a long time while I was singing. He said she looked like a normal person - NOT a spirit. He said that she had no wrinkles on her face, NOT cripple and was standing straight up holding her hands behind her back and looking at all who were there including him. I don't understand a lot about the afterlife BUT

I know my MOM definitely lives on. She probably wanted to let us know that SHE HAS ALREADY RISEN.

Jun 2, 2014, 6:05 PM

My husband, I and our 4-year old son lived in Oak Park, MI. One night my son fell asleep in our room. While my husband and son were sleeping, I awakened and saw a splatter of blood on my husband's forehead and another splatter of blood on my son's forehead. One of the prayers I pray is, "May the blood of Jesus Christ cover over [names]." I believe that was the Lord allowing me to see what the enemy sees when he sees those who belong to Jesus Christ.

Summer 2004

Every time I play the song We Cry Holy by Deitrick Haddon, Jason Champion and Voices Of Unity, my broken speaker starts working! I am still in worship from the ALL-night SHUT-IN service last night from 10PM-6AM this morning. Glory to God! Worship Flow! I feel SO inspired.

Jun 28, 2014, 3:28 PM

Dawn Kellum is feeling happy.

I was just about to go back to sleep this morning and miss my class this morning at church until I heard a bird directly outside my bedroom window chirping almost ENDLESSLY. I could NOT go back to sleep. Obedience is better than sacrifice.

Dec 14, 2014, 8:06 AM

Dawn Kellum updated her status.

I was headed to work this morning, but a part of my van got stuck in my driveway's ditch so I shoveled almost 2 feet of snow to try to get out. I STILL couldn't get out and almost fell on the ice. It was DARK out too. I was exhausted!

I then swallowed my pride and awoke my husband to tell him I was stuck. He QUICKLY came out of the house, quickly shoveled the rest of the snow and quickly LIFTED AND PUSHED that part of the car OUT the ditch. I then went inside to fix my lunch for work and had a voicemail on my phone. NO WORK TODAY.

LESSON LEARNED: Check your phone FIRST before leaving out. Humble yourself and ASK FOR HELP.

Feb 2, 2015, 7:25 PM

Dawn Kellum is feeling loved.

...just prayed, "God, please let your angels encamp around me and [my children] while we sleep." Then suddenly I heard a very loud creaking sound on my kitchen floor that offsets my bedroom like an angel or angels landed on my kitchen floor!

May 14, 2015, 12:30 AM

What kind of Lord is this where even the computer obeys His voice!?

I was here in tears staring at my mom's picture and SUD-DENLY my CLOSED laptop randomly goes off and says the following:

"God was David's power source. He confessed that the Lord was His strength. David was a man of prayer and worship. He enjoyed the Lord's presence. The Lord's presence was David's source of joy and strength. His songs were powerful, prophetic weapons against the enemy. There is no substitute for a life of prayer and worship."

I don't know how YouTube even got to this video while the laptop was CLOSED and why is my closed laptop going off at 7 am when it was off ALL NIGHT!!??? I got the message God. Thank you God.

Oct 10, 2015, 8:14 AM

My day yesterday involved a hard hat, safety goggles, ear plugs, boots, a respirator, water, extreme heights, walking on train tracks, a forceful wind that blew me away, barbecue beef briskets, gourmet popcorn, tunnels, winding stairwells, jet engines, high catwalks, deep water and then good music and fun times with my babies. I'm so grateful for my place of employment, great co-workers and my babies. I love my life right now.

Feb 27, 2016, 7:38 AM

Dawn Kellum is feeling silly.

Random thought: There's probably someone right now on Facebook trolling and hating while picking their buggers and eating them. Stop hating. It's okay to show love.

Apr 24, 2017, 10:58 PM

Dawn Kellum is feeling shocked.

Random: If clothing will be left here after the Rapture, will weaves, wigs, extensions and more be left in random places?

Aug 3, 2017, 8:25 AM

....when the store sells a part of your children's new bedroom furniture because you had to wait to get a truck to get the rest of it and still God makes a way for the person who bought the furniture to apologize and have you pick up the rest of the furniture on a street called GRACE.

Then you see a long lost childhood friend at the same store you experienced this at who is very happy to see you. God bless you Tracy R.

God keeps doing great things for me. What else does God have in store for me?? I thank God for favor.

Nov 12, 2017, 7:26 AM

Coincidence?

1. My husband & I went out to eat to celebrate our anniversary. All of the restaurants in the area either were too crowded or wouldn't see us. We finally found one with GOOD food AND service by a waiter who went above and beyond named Christian.
2. I created a support ticket with an international vendor to help with a major and very difficult upgrade for work. The name of the engineer, out of thousands, assigned to my case was Cristian. He also went way above and beyond.

Mar 27, 2018, 10:31 PM

The Lord asked me to post the article listening and hearing from God on my blog before I went to sleep last night. I fell asleep anyway and one of THE loudest roars of THUNDER WOKE ME UP AT ABOUT 4AM SO I FINISHED AND POSTED the article. Amen.

Oct 5, 2013, 7:44 AM

My daughter had a "Door Knocker" project for her school that gives experience with the Engineering Design Process (Brainstorming, Design, Create, Test, Improve). The door knocker must contain the right materials so, once motion energy converts to sound energy, it can be heard throughout the whole house. How can this be used in a parable from a biblical standpoint? Energy transference, maybe? Is God knocking at the door of your heart, maybe? Are you listening, hunh?

Oct 6, 2019, 9:42 PM

Dawn Kellum is feeling ashamed.

Elderly woman: "It's much warmer out today. Isn't it?"

Me: "Yes. It was warm enough for me to ride my bike to work today - about 3 1/2 miles. It was beautiful although I had to walk some of the way."

Elderly woman: "That's great. My friend and I normally ride 10 miles when we go. It normally takes us about an hour. Walking slows you down though."

Me (thinking): (Wow. I'm probably about 30 years younger than this elderly lady. My 3 1/2 mile bike ride/"forced to walk due to intermittent exhaustion" to work took about an hour)

Me to my husband: "Honey, I feel really bad. I really thought I was doing something."

Hubby and I: Cracks up laughing. (I'm feeling shameful at the same time.)

Nov 20, 2019, 5:50 PM

Me: (smells popcorn after 9PM and notices it's my tween's microwave popcorn) "Who got popcorn this late? You know you can have problems with your heart lying down on all that grease. It's not good for you."

My tween: "Well, Mommy, it's readily available in the kitchen so I got some."

me: (angry) Crack is also readily available in this neighborhood. That doesn't mean you indulge. (cracks up laughing like where did that statement come from?!) My children keep me "on my toes."

Dec 9, 2019, 9:31 PM

One of my daughters' hair routines:

1. Wash hair with Sulfur 8 shampoo to help maintain PH balance, perform deep cleaning and more
2. Condition and moisturize hair with Crème of Nature curl activator crème
3. Separate and detangle hair while damp with detangling comb

4. Place separated, detangled hair into Bantu knots while continuing to separate and detangle the remaining hair

5. Unravel and Blow dry, with comb attachment, each separated Bantu knot

6. Section first part of hair to be braided. Place remaining hair in plastic clamps.

7. Apply Smooth and Shine Extra Hold around the sectioned hair to be braided

8. "Fine-separate" sectioned hair to be braided again for neatness

9. Under-braid with feed-in braid method using pre-feathered, pre-stretched long extension color #1 hair

10. Continue Steps 7 - 9 until hair is fully sectioned, "smoothed," "fine-separated" and braided using the under-braid feed-in method

11. Boil water and then pour water into cup

12. Place ends of extension hair into the cup of boiling water and then pat with a dry towel until cooled

13. Ensure daughter is happy with hair or a redo may be necessary

Feb 2, 2020, 12:53 AM

Dawn Kellum is feeling embarrassed.

Thank God it's Friday. I had to give my daughter something important and accidentally flashed her 8th Grade Zoom this morning with some clothes on of course and looking a pure hot mess - my "au naturale" granny Mom look. Lol!! I didn't realize what I was doing until she screamed under a whisper, "Mommy, you're in the camera!" I immediately apologized and told her, "You should've warned me!"

Aug 28, 2020, 9:25 AM

I went into Walmart today. I get out of my car & go into the store. I didn't notice ANY thing weird like googly eyes, someone following me, etc. I was in the store a while and when I came OUT I saw a little piece of paper stuck in the door that said "CALL BIG ROCK" with a telephone number on it. I opened the door and let that foolishness fly in the wind.

Remember that God loves you the most out of anybody you knew or EVER will know. Don't be deceived. There are a lot of BIG ROCKs out there. They ONLY want to take your youth and leave you diseased and out of your head. That way they can throw you away like trash, abuse & misuse you and leave you all alone and CRAZY. But JESUS is the one that LOVES you SO much to clean you up, heal you, and put you BACK in your right mind because you actually started to KEEP your mind stayed on him.

Apr 29, 2013, 8:31 PM

I took the children to the mall for much needed shoe shopping. We went past a store with a HUMAN MANNEQUIN in the window! I had to take a DOUBLE take and thought I was seeing things until SHE shifted her eyes. I then told my son to look at the mannequin (he didn't know she was real LOL) He looked and stared for a long time until she waved slowly at him and smiled. HE JUMPED Back IN UTTER SHOCK!

Insight: Understand that everything is not what it appears to be! Be not deceived.

Nov 22, 2013, 9:20 PM

The Unseen Force.

After I had my 2nd-born child (my rainbow baby) in 2017, I was resting on my bed in my room on the Eastside of Lansing during my 6-8 week recovery after giving birth via C-Section. The window was cracked open to allow air to circulate throughout the room. As I was resting, I suddenly awakened to an unseen force pulling me off the bed - my feet first. Although the light was off in the room, I could still see very clearly in the room. There was nobody in the room that I could physically see pulling me. I immediately called, "Jesus!" It stopped. I proceeded to pray and anoint the rooms and that NEVER happened again!

The Red Man
LOCATION - LANSING, MI
AGE - Toddler

When I was a toddler, one of my older brothers told me that he walked outside and saw me wondering down the dirt road by our house in a daze following a red figure. He later described that red figure as having the outline of a human. The inside of the figure was filled with red lights. It appeared as if it were floating.

While I was in this apparent daze, a sibling called me; but, he mentioned that I was not responding and was rather fixated on this floating red figure that seemed to drift down the road. Finally, my brother was able to quickly get the attention of other family members and bring me back home to safety.

Strangely, my parents told me a few years later that, around the same time, there were many occurrences of child abductions in that same region. Understand that some child abductors use witchcraft to abduct children.

The Red Man Returns

LOCATION - EAST LANSING, MI

AGE - Freshman in College, 18 years old

In 1993, I enrolled at MSU (Michigan State University) to major in the field of Engineering Arts. I had the privilege of staying in one of the University's dormitories that primarily housed those of freshman status. I shared a room with an African-American girl from Romulus. She was all about keeping up appearances and wondering what people thought about her. I was more concerned with getting an education, minding my business and pleasing God. She also had what appeared to be a vampire sense when it came to smelling things. She would complain often of various suspicious odors. She obviously had problems with my hygiene. She was the chief apostle of supposed cleanliness. Over time, I became more self-conscious in making sure that I and all of my little area and person were not giving off any suspicious odors.

One late night while my roommate was out, I burned incense in the room to burn off any potential odors that could have been lingering in the room. My favorite incense at the time was African Violet. I thought that was the best smelling scent ever. I was enjoying the aroma of this heavenly scent so much that I walked around my bed and applied the ashes of it to the circumference of the bed so that I could smell it while I slept. I was careful not to apply hot ashes on my bed covers. Once my roommate arrived back home, I wanted there to be no complaints in regards to ferocious odors. Who wouldn't like the aromatic scent of African Violet?

It was very late once she returned. I was already in bed heading to sleep, facing my wall and minding my own business. I didn't care where she came from. I just didn't want to hear her sassy mouth complaining about suspicious smells. Thankfully, she did not complain that night about odors. She quickly went to her bed and went to sleep. No complaining. Yes! Approximately one hour later, I woke up out of a very light sleep and felt a presence standing by my bed. I was scared to turn around; however, I mustered up enough strength to finally turn around. I looked around and saw the same red figure I had followed as a toddler. This was the same exact figure standing in my college dormitory almost 15 years later! I was terrified; however, I was taught by my Dad to call on the name of Jesus in any emergency situations. As loud as I could, I screamed, "Jesus!" The figure immediately left. My roommate must have been drunk or high because she barely looked up towards my direction and immediately went back to sleep.

Since that night, I had no more visits from that specific apparition.

The Everlasting Shadow
LOCATION - LANSING, MI
AGE - Teenager
There was something back in the day called the Jheri Curl.

If your ethnic hair was hard to deal with, you were given the option to place it into an easy to manage state. One option was to apply a relaxer that relaxed your hair texture into a straight form. Another option was to apply something called the jheri curl which relaxed your hair texture into a semi-permanent curl pattern. I was grateful to have a cousin and a sister at the church that was skilled enough to do a jheri curl. I was so excited when they placed my moderately textured hair into the managed jheri curl state. I wouldn't have to get it done again for another 3 months. I would wear a curl bag at night and wake up in the morning and be ready to go about my day without spending too much time in the morning doing my hair before school or church. One may need to put some curl activator and moisturizer on their hair in order to define the curls better; however, a jheri curl was still very easy to maintain.

My bedroom was the first one on the right once you go up the second set of wooden stairs. In my bedroom was a small closet. The door to the closet was painted white and blue. The majority of the closet door was painted white. The rectangular blocks on the door were painted light blue. I would often stand next to that specific closet door while getting clothes out of the closet and occasionally see the shadow of my head near the top of the door. The shadow displayed the outline of my face along with my hair within the curl bag.

One night I was headed to sleep while facing the opposite direction of my closet door which was barely open. I turned my body around to change positions in my bed and noticed something very odd affixed to the closet door. The same shadow I normally saw while standing at the door was the same shadow I beheld while I laid in my bed. I immediately became terrified. I assumed it was probably the shadow from an object in my room being projected from the light in the bathroom that was in diagonal position from my room. I moved my hand towards my bedroom door to see if moving the door would cause the shadow to move. The shadow did not move at all. That shadow NEVER moved. It appeared to be stuck there. I then said my nightly prayers again and finally fell asleep. The shadow stayed on the door for years.

The Dancing Blue Man
LOCATION - MERIDIAN TOWNSHIP TOWNHOME
AGE - 30s

My husband and I had finally moved to the township we desired. Founded in the early 1800's along the Grand River as a trading point, Meridian Township residents enjoy quiet, safe, and well maintained neighborhoods with plenty of parks, pathways, and recreation. With natural beauty on roads, interurban pathways, and vibrant business districts, Meridian Township is a great atmosphere for families.

A strange occurrence happened while we lived in one of Meridian Township's most beautiful townhomes. We had been living there for a few months. My youngest two children had a night light in their room that projected shadows of cartoon characters onto the walls. The older of my youngest two children complained about a man coming in her room at night. She described it as if it were a spirit. My room was across from theirs so I would watch their room throughout the night and didn't see what they were referring to. I still proceeded to anoint all four corners of their walls with blessed oil and say, "May the blood of Jesus Christ cover." I was also led by the Holy Spirit to remove the night light that projected shadows of cartoon characters onto the walls. My two youngest children complained no more about a man coming into their room at night.

A few months later, I started to use the night light for my room. I enjoyed watching the cartoon characters project onto the ceiling. My family and I were sleeping peacefully at night. One day I went to the local video store to rent a horror film. I could sense the Holy Spirit telling me not to get it; however, I continued to get it. I thought it would be entertaining to watch a scary movie with my family. Once I returned home, I didn't watch the movie immediately. I was debating on whether I would watch it or not.

One night as I was sleeping in the bed with my husband, I looked up at the cartoon characters that were projected onto the ceiling. In the midst of the projected cartoon characters formed the shape of a bluish shadowy figure in the form of a man. I saw this blue shadowy creature dancing within the cartoon characters on my ceiling! I immediately called on the name of JESUS. Immediately, it slithered slowly across the ceiling and down the wall and through my bedroom door. I remember seeing its hand slither out the door.

I then said a nightly prayer "Lord, please let your angels encamp around me and my family as we sleep in Jesus name. Let your blood cover over us in Jesus name." I and all my household were able to sleep peaceably again.

Now, one of the most bizarre things happened a few days later once we actually started to watch that horror movie I recently rented from the video store. None of us knew anything about the movie other than what was written and visible on the outer cover of the DVD. The movie summary on the DVD and the images did not mention or portray blue apparitions at all.

We eventually put the movie into the DVD player to watch the movie together as a family. A few moments into the movie I saw the SAME blue shadowy creature I had saw slither across my ceiling begin to slither through a man's window in this movie nigh unto his bedside! I immediately jumped up in sheer terror and said to my husband and family "TURN IT OFF NOW!" I returned that DVD back to the store with the quickness.

Massive Demonic Oppression
LOCATION - DETROIT, MI
AGE- 20s

The following multiple occurrences happened while I stayed in a blue and green house on the West side of Detroit, MI less than one block from the infamous Linwood street. These happened during a time I was starting to get back into fellowship with Jesus Christ. I had gotten weak spiritually and was coming back into fellowship with my Lord and Savior; however, I was still in the valley of decision.

I was asleep one night and woke up to a poltergeist in the form of what appeared to be a dark tunnel or black hole. I immediately called on the name of Jesus and it went away.

I awoke one night to a boy in a baseball hat standing next to the light in my room with boots on. It looked as if he believed that was his room; however, he just turned the light on in our room and just stood there looking at my husband and I. I called on the name of Jesus and he left.

I awoke one morning to find my bed encompassed with huge out-of-this-world bugs ALL OVER ME AND MY BED. I immediately called on the name of Jesus and it went away. This happened a lot. I knew they weren't physical bugs because I never had any bites (smile).

Another morning I awoke to a hideous demon that had the form of a woman with multiple snake tongues. I immediately called on the name of Jesus and it went away.

The Medusa Demon
LOCATION - DETROIT MI - THE LITTLE HOUSE
AGE - 20s

My husband and I lived in a cozy one-bedroom apartment with our young son. We were blessed to have a place to lay our heads at night until we could afford something better. We went through hard times. At one point, I needed new clothes and couldn't afford to buy them so I scheduled an appointment with a local soup kitchen that provided food and clothing. I was thankful to have such an opportunity. I would wear those clothes well. I remember bringing a big bag of clothes home. They weren't new; but, they were new and fresh to me. I remember taking them to the Laundromat and washing them before I wore them. I then proceeded to place them in their several destinations within my closet and chest drawers.

One night as I slept, I awoke to a hideous demon that looked similar to the Greek mythological creature medusa. It had a huge snake tongue and had massive deformities. It was scaly and looked monstrous and hateful. I called on the name of Jesus Christ and it immediately went away.

Now, this was when I first noticed that my son also had the ability to see the paranormal. One night we were watching television and enjoying our family time together in the living room. The one-bedroom apartment was so small. You could easily look down the hall past the bathroom on the left towards the bedroom while sitting in the living room. That night my son, who was 4 at the time, looked toward the bedroom and, in sheer terror, he uttered, "There's two ladies in the room." I immediately thought "Hmmm. That's wonderful. He can see angels."

He then began to describe them. He described the SAME demon I saw a few nights ago hovering over me with the snake tongue. He described it exactly. Oddly enough, he said it was two of them rather than one!

I was still learning about casting out demons and taking authority over demonic warfare. Hence, for some time, my son and I lodged with one of my elder sisters. My husband stayed back at the little house to 'toughen it out'. I wasn't experienced with that type of warfare so I consulted my Dad. He is a powerful and anointed man of God who has blessed many houses throughout his lifetime and cast out many demons. Many people have been healed, including me, through his "laying-on" of hands by the power of Jesus Christ. I made a promise that, once my Dad taught me that time to cast demons out of my house, I would not call him again to do it. I would DO IT MYSELF or my husband would do it. I wanted the power to command peace over my home.

Once my Mom and Dad finally arrived, my family and I were elated. We were finally going to sleep peaceably.

My Dad began by asking us if we had recently brought anything into the house like clothes, furniture, etc. I immediately answered him by mentioning the clothes I had recently acquired from the soup kitchen. I felt hurt because I knew that I would, more than likely, have to get rid of them. He read scripture and proceeded in blessing the house with his blessed oil - all four corners of each room. He cast out the demons according to how Jesus Christ did in New Testament scripture. It was very simple and short. It was only a few minutes. From that point on, we had no more problems with those demons. Thank you Jesus!

The Mumbler

LOCATION - HASLETT, MI

AGE - nearly 40

My sister-in-law succumbed to a grave illness October 14, 2013. Before she passed, I would go over there and minister to her, encourage her, take care of the house, pray, sing to her and more. Every time I would go over her house to help out, she would call my name a lot. I loved her dearly and wanted to be a help. Her mobility was hindered sometime before her passing so I would take time to go over there and help her to the bathroom and much more. I remember her calling to me for her special pink cup of ice cold water and I would run swiftly to the freezer to acquire it and return back to help her drink it. A few days after she passed, I remembered how much she would call me so I made the statement to many loved ones that "I really miss her voice."

A few days after her funeral, I was lying in bed one night and awakened to the sound of a woman's voice mumbling next to my bedside. I looked over there and did not see anything or anyone so I called on the name of Jesus Christ and it immediately went away.

CHAPTER 19

Pray and Don't Worry

The Prayers that satan hates

14 March, 2014

I normally do not post many articles about satan because Jesus Christ is Lord of all and reigns on the throne and our minds and speech should have JESUS CHRIST IN and ON THEM; however, it is important to understand the power that exists in certain types of prayer that STOPS the devil's plans and assignments in OUR LIVES AND OUR WORLD and BREAKS the CHAINS of the ENEMY.

The following was gathered from the Divine Revelations site and gives accounts from the testimony of a past human satanic agent who is NOW A BORN-AGAIN CHRISTIAN. Hallelujah! He talks about certain types of prayers that STOP the devil's plans and assignments in your life AND OTHERS AND REMOVES BONDAGE from your LIFE AND OTHERS.

He states that your prayers appear in the following forms:

1. Some prayers appear like smoke that drifts along and vanishes in the air. These prayers come from people who have SIN in their lives that they are not willing to deal with. Their prayers are very WEAK; they are blown away and disappear in the air.

2. Another type of prayer is also like smoke. It rises upward until it reaches the rock; it cannot break through the rock. These prayers usually come from people who try to purify themselves, but who lack faith as they pray. They usually ignore the other important aspects that are needed when someone prays.

3. The third type of prayer is like smoke that is filled with fire. As it rises upward, it is so hot that when it reaches the rock, the rock begins to melt like wax. It pierces the rock and goes through.

Many times, as people begin to pray, their prayers look like the first type. But as they continue praying, their prayers change and become like the second type of prayer. And as they continue praying, suddenly their prayers ignite into FLAMES. Their prayers become so powerful that they pierce through the rock.

Many times evil agents would notice that prayers were changing and coming very close to becoming fire. These agents would then communicate with other spirits on earth and tell them, "Distract that person from prayer. Stop them from praying. Pull them out."

Many times Christians yield to these distractions. They are pressing through, repenting and allowing the Word to check their spirit. Their faith is growing. Their prayers are becoming more focused. Then the devil notices that their prayers are gaining strength, and the distractions begin. Telephones ring. Sometimes, in the middle of very, very intense prayer, the telephone rings and you think you can go answer it and then come back and continue praying. However, when you return, you go back to the beginning. And that's what the devil wants.

Other kinds of distractions come your way. They may touch your body, bringing pain somewhere. They may make you hungry, causing you to want to go to the kitchen to prepare something to eat. As long as they can get you out of that place, they have defeated you. He said to the pastors,

"Teach the people to set aside some time, not just for some casual praying, they can do that the rest of the day. Once a day, they should have a time when they are focusing wholeheartedly on God, without any distractions. "

If the people persist in this kind of prayer and allow themselves to be inspired in the spirit and to keep going, something happens in the spirit. The fire touches that rock, and it melts. The man said that when the melting begins, it is so hot that no demon spirit can stand it. No human spirit can stand it. They all flee. They all run away.

There comes an opening in the spiritual realm. As soon as it appears, all this trouble in prayer stops. The person who is praying on the ground feels like their prayer has suddenly become so smooth, so enjoyable, so powerful and intense. I've discovered that at that moment, we normally lose all awareness of time and other things. Not that we become disorderly; God takes care of our time. But it is as if you lay down everything, and hook up with God. The man said that when the prayers break through, from that moment on there is no resistance at all, and the person praying can continue as long as he wants. There is no resistance to stop him.

Then he said that after the person finishes praying, the hole remains open. He said that when people rise from their place of prayer, and move on, the open hole moves along with them. They are no longer operating under the blanket. They are operating under an open heaven. He said that in that state, the devil cannot do what he wants against them.

The presence of the Lord is like a pillar from heaven resting on their lives. They are protected, and there is so much power inside the pillar that as they move around, the presence touches other people as well. It discerns what the enemy has done in other people. And as they talk to people who are standing with them, they too come inside the pillar.

As long as they stay inside the pillar, all the bondages placed on them by the enemy weaken.

Dawn Kellum updated her status.

Take time to pray especially this week and in this season. Be mindful of prayer distractions and offenses sent to discourage you or cause you to have bitterness, hatred, un-forgiveness and more that stops your prayers.

Oct 27, 2020, 9:47 AM

Dawn Kellum updated her status.

Do not be anxious about anything, but in everything by prayer and supplication with thanksgiving let your requests be made known to God. And the peace of God, which surpasses all understanding, will guard your hearts and your minds in Christ Jesus. Philippians 4:6-7

Oct 27, 2014, 7:21 AM

Dawn Kellum updated her status.

James 5:16 (KJV) Confess your faults one to another, and pray one for another, that ye may be healed. The effectual fervent prayer of a righteous man availeth much.

Jun 18, 2014, 7:09 AM

11/9/19 -I danced. Insider. You Had To Be There. This was a powerful Women's Conference.

Nov 10, 2019, 5:04 PM

To all of us affected by the automotive shutdown, God will take care of us and make a way. We should pray and not worry. Tough times require much prayer and God's Holy Spirit to comfort us.

Sep 17, 2019, 6:04 PM

Prayerlessness = breathlessness. The absence of prayer to the life source is like a human being without oxygen (source of life). When I had a heart attack, the increase in oxygen helped to stop the breathlessness. Pray without ceasing.

Nov 9, 2016, 5:35 AM

God's word: we wrestle not against flesh & blood but spiritual wickedness in high places, etc. This is a spiritual war that is fought through prayer. Fight this war through prayer

Satan: I need to come up with a strategy to prevent a whole body of believers from getting a prayer through by causing them to become offended by the inexcusable thereby allowing un-forgiveness to enter and stay.

God's word: we wrestle not against flesh & blood but spiritual wickedness in high places. Fight this war through prayer. If you don't forgive others who trespass against you, neither will your Father in Heaven forgive you your trespasses.

Jul 7, 2016, 6:23 AM

Thank you Jesus for another day. I am still trusting, still standing, fighting the good fight and still praying. God is the same yesterday, today and forevermore. I enter your gates with Thanksgiving and your courts with praise and bless your name. Thank you so much for your grace. Great is thy faithfulness. Our Father who art in Heaven hallowed be thy name thy kingdom come Thy will be done on earth as it is in Heaven Give us this day our daily bread and forgive us our debts as we forgive our debtors Lead us not into temptation [to sin or blaspheme your holy name] but deliver us from evil for thine is the kingdom and the power and the glory forever. Father in Jesus Christ name please let your angels encamp round about me and my friends, family and loved ones everywhere we go. Please keep us from all hurt, harm, danger seen and unseen. I give you all my cares, issues and worries. Please keep me from evil.

May the blood of Jesus Christ cover me and my loved ones

in Christ Jesus name. Whatever role or profession I operate in please guide me with your divine wisdom and more as I surrender all to you my blessed Savior. I love you always Jesus. Satan the Lord Jesus Christ rebuke you and Remove your hands off me and [mention names] in the name of Jesus Christ. Jesus Christ is Lord and has all power in His hands. None is greater than He.

Dec 12, 2017, 7:04 AM

...up early praying for my family and all those in the path of these storms, fires, wars, floods, devastation and all suffering hardship...

Sep 10, 2017, 4:19 AM

The lightning and raindrops on the window got me up and interrupted a dream of me holding hands with friends praying. I was even still praying as I awakened AND when I woke up. Thank God for a praying spirit.

Jul 7, 2017, 4:22 AM

God doesn't always answer prayers the way we want, but He is not like humans who break promises. He is true to His word. Trust His plan. Hallelujah

Jun 21, 2017, 6:29 AM

Pray for the world. We are in a fractured creation.

Jun 7, 2017, 6:57 AM

Reminder: God is in control of your situations. Don't worry or act crazy. Pray for direction. Be encouraged.

May 25, 2017, 12:55 PM

When God lays it on your heart to pray for someone PLEASE do so. Be encouraged. Have a Blessed day all.

Oct 27, 2015, 6:56 AM

FATHER, IN THE NAME OF JESUS CHRIST OF NAZARETH, MY MASTER, DELIVERER, STRONG TOWER AND POWER, I ask you to keep the same hedge of protection around my family, my mind, my heart, my emotions, my ministry and my relationship with You. The same hedge You put on Job. Father, in the name of Jesus, I ask You to keep an encampment of Your powerful angels to surround my loved ones, my ministry, my family and me every day. Father, in the name of Jesus, I ask You to send a host of ministering angels to attend to our hurts, our needs, our pain and our infirmities, to strengthen us in every season of our lives.

Father, I praise You and thank You that Your glory is my rear guard. In the name of Jesus, I ask You to surround my loved ones, my ministry and me with a supernatural wall of fire. Protect me from any assault of the evil one. Father, in the name of Jesus, I claim Your promise to be my shield and protector always. In the unmatchable name of Jesus Christ, I command my thoughts and my thinking to be under the obedience of Christ Jesus, Amen.

Oct 29, 2018, 8:53 AM

..inspired by Franklin Graham. We as Christians should be praying for our president and our leaders every day out of obedience to the Scriptures. It is a biblical command that we are to obey. "I exhort therefore, that, first of all, supplications, prayers, intercessions, and giving of thanks, be made for all men; For kings, and for all that are in authority; that we may lead a quiet and peaceable life in all godliness and honesty" (1 Timothy 2:1-2, KJV).

We know from Scripture that God can turn the hearts of kings (Proverbs 21:1). That means that we should be praying for God's will to be done and for our leaders to seek God and listen to Him. We should pray that they would be surrounded by godly counsel and, most important, that our leadership would personally know God and the salvation found through faith in Jesus Christ alone.

We should be diligently praying that God would give our president, Congress and military leaders wisdom. Our senators and governors and council members need our prayers—even if you did not vote for them. Even if you did vote for them, their decisions can be easily swayed by spiritual warfare. This gives us another reason to pray for ALL of them!

There should be a sense of urgency in our prayer life, an understanding that we "do not wrestle against flesh and blood, but against principalities, against powers, against the rulers of the darkness of this age, against spiritual hosts of wickedness in the heavenly places" (Ephesians 6:12). The prince of darkness is grimly and powerfully at work in world affairs, and prayer is a great battlefield especially as we pray for those in leadership.

The "king's heart is in the hand of the Lord, like the rivers of water" (Proverbs 21:1). This means that a Sovereign God can turn the heart of a king at any time and in any way. Neither kings, nor presidents, nor mayors, nor members of Congress are the ultimate authority—God is. Reference (Psalm 2:2-4) - Credit to Franklin Graham

Nov 6, 2018, 9:37 AM

Father, I take back in the name of Jesus everything that the cankerworm and the locust have eaten from my life and my loved ones lives in Jesus name. I pour fire upon every devil's head and every unclean spirit and every witch that has risen up against my family, my spouse, my children, my finances, my church and me. I smite them with the blood of Jesus seven times and destroy them never to rise again in Jesus Christ name.

Oct 24, 2018, 7:45 AM

I burn down the banners and scrolls of any evil plan that they have against me and my family and my ministry, in Jesus' name.

I call the fire of God to fall upon the enemy's camp and destroy every demonic altar that has my name on it, in Jesus' name.

I call upon the Holy Spirit right now to make me invisible in the spirit realm, as well as my family, my ministry and my loved ones, so that the devil and his demons cannot find me/ us

Oct 23, 2018, 12:06 PM

Dawn Kellum updated her status.
I ask the Holy Spirit, in the name of Jesus Christ, to give

me insight into the evil plans of the witches, the sorcerers and the warlocks that are against my family, my ministry and my life. Let those plans be destroyed in Jesus' name.

I rebuke and dismantle every plan or any insight that the devil and his demons have against me. Let them be destroyed in Jesus' name.

I send confusion into the enemy's camp right now in Jesus' name.

I send arrows dipped in the blood of Jesus Christ right now into the enemy's camp, in Jesus' name.

Oct 23, 2018, 12:06 PM

AFTER HANGING UP THE PHONE, LEAVING WORK, GROCERY STORE, NEIGHBORS, OR VISITORS LEAVE YOUR HOME, ETC., PRAY THIS IMMEDIATELY:

IN JESUS NAME, I COMMAND EVERY DEMON THAT HAS FOLLOWED ME, WAS SENT TO ME, OR TRANSFERRED TO ME, TO LEAVE ME NOW.

Oct 19, 2018, 7:12 AM

Dawn Kellum updated her status.

WHEN ENTERING YOUR OFFICE, GROCERY STORE, ANYONE ELSE'S HOME, ETC., PRAY THIS BEFORE ENTERING:

IN JESUS CHRIST NAME, I COVER MYSELF AND THIS PLACE WITH THE BLOOD OF JESUS. I BIND UP EVERY DEMON IN HERE, AND I ASK FOR GIANT WARRIOR ANGELS TO PROTECT ME/US.

Oct 19, 2018, 7:11 AM

Dawn Kellum updated her status.

IN JESUS NAME, I CUT AND BURN ALL UN-GODLY SILVER CORDS AND LAY LINES. AS YOUR WAR CLUB AND WEAPONS OF WAR, I BREAK DOWN, UNDAM, AND BLOW UP ALL WALLS OF PROTECTION AROUND ALL WITCHES, WAR-LOCKS, WIZARDS, SATANISTS, SORCERERS, AND THE LIKE, AND I BREAK THE POWER OF ALL CURSES, HEXES, VEXES, SPELLS, CHARMS, FETISHES, PSYCHIC PRAYERS, PSYCHIC THOUGHTS, ALL WITCHCRAFT, SORCERY, MAGIC, VOODOO, ALL MIND CONTROL, JINXES, POTIONS, BEWITCHMENTS, DEATH, DESTRUC-TION, SICKNESS, PAIN, TORMENT, PSYCHIC POWER, PSYCHIC WARFARE, PRAYER CHAINS, IN-CENSE AND CANDLE BURNING, INCANTATIONS, CHANTING, UNGODLY BLESSINGS, HOODOO, CRYSTALS, ROOTWORKS, AND EVERYTHING ELSE BEING SENT MY WAY, OR MY FAMILY MEMBER'S WAY, OR MY FRIENDS OR ANY DELIVERANCE MIN-ISTRIES WAY, AND I RETURN IT, AND THE DEMONS TO THE SENDER, ONE HUNDREDFOLD, AND I BIND IT TO THEM BY THE BLOOD OF JESUS.

Oct 18, 2018, 7:03 AM

Dawn Kellum updated her status.

Father, In Jesus' Name, I take the Blood of Jesus Christ and break the power of all witches, warlocks, wizards, sa-tanists, sorcerers, wiccans, pagans, and any other source, and all of their rituals off of all of us. With the Blood of Jesus Christ, I erase all evil lines drawn on any parts of our body, soul, will, and emotions.

Oct 18, 2018, 6:59 AM

The Lord told me yesterday on the way to church, "Your prayers now will affect your future later."

Jul 13, 2020, 7:43 AM

Matthew 6

9 After this manner therefore pray ye: Our Father which art in heaven, Hallowed be thy name.

10 Thy kingdom come. Thy will be done in earth, as it is in heaven.

11 Give us this day our daily bread.

12 And forgive us our debts, as we forgive our debtors.

13 And lead us not into temptation, but deliver us from evil: For thine is the kingdom, and the power, and the glory, forever. Amen. 14For if ye forgive men their trespasses, your heavenly Father will also forgive you:

15 But if ye forgive not men their trespasses, neither will your Father forgive your trespasses.

Nov 10, 2020, 7:18 AM

Father I pray in the name of Jesus Christ that you will help me to be a woman UN-spotted in your eyes and an example of YOUR righteousness - not mine. MY righteousness is like a bunch of FILTHY rags.. Amen

Jun 1, 2013, 9:50 AM

Father, I pray in the name of Jesus Christ that you will please allow me to be an example of your righteousness ALL day today and serve your purpose for me by the authority of Jesus Christ my Lord and Savior. Amen.

Jun 1, 2013, 9:44 AM

...getting prepared as a Prayer Warrior/Intercessor for my Pastor and friends heading to Ghana, West Africa this weekend...and still being faithful at Church

Aug 8, 2013, 8:50 PM

I see God's kingdom coming on earth. Don't stop praying y'all.

Aug 28, 2013, 6:18 PM

...Up early praying and meditating. I hear the chains falling in the spiritual realm. He whom the Son sets free is FREE indeed

Sep 28, 2013, 5:33 AM

Father, we need you now Lord during this very difficult time. My family member was given a few days to live.

Sep 28, 2013, 5:51 AM

There are powerful prayers in the book "Bondage Breaker" by Neil T. Andersen

Oct 3, 2013, 7:04 AM

Don't worry about tomorrow. PRAISE the One who holds Tomorrow today.

Sep 28, 2013, 4:44 AM

When you receive God's Holy Spirit and live a life of submission to Jesus Christ, you have power to cast out demons and evil spirits in the name of Jesus Christ. Many people in this nation, including some professed Christians, have demons and evil spirits. Cast them demons out, come against those evil and unclean spirits and command that they be removed from you. Sometimes you have to do this multiple times in a day. Holy Spirit discernment is needed to expose the type of demon, evil or unclean spirit you or others have.

Jul 15, 2020, 9:15 AM

CHAPTER 20

Thy Will be Done

Stress makes you believe that everything has to happen right now. Faith reassures you that everything will happen in God's timing - unknown

Calm down and pray.

Jan 15, 2015, 9:19 PM

Sometimes God closes doors because it's time to move forward. He knows you won't move unless your circumstances force you. Trust Him!

Apr 15, 2014, 5:38 PM

..through life's uncertainties Give Me Jesus. You can have the whole world but give me Jesus.

Apr 25, 2016, 11:39 PM

God please help us to see your will for us and help us to walk in it.

Sep 18, 2015, 7:02 AM

God's will = God's way + God's timing VS my will = my

way + my timing. ONLY God is all- knowing and all-seeing -so His will be done. Hallelujah and Amen

Dec 9, 2015, 6:51 AM

Dawn Kellum updated her status.

Reminder to the child of God: Your life is in God's hand. Your entire life is being orchestrated by God. Say "Use Me God." I Trust God's Plan although I'm out of my comfort zone. This is the life of a child of God. Know who you are. Did you know your son-ship changed so that your master is God Almighty!

Jan 13, 2016, 8:25 AM

...Word to those who minister for God to people. We are not supposed to minister through words, song, dance, playing music, etc. to bring glory to ourselves, get men or women to our bedsides or for people to see how sexy we are in front of the public. God gave us the gift to glorify Him and not ourselves. Don't be like lucifer people. All Glory to God. Amen

Dec 3, 2016, 8:49 PM

The greatest mystery writer-God. I gotta' run on to see what the rest of the story is gonna' be...but I gotta' trust God through it all because He wrote the book.

May 12, 2016, 6:59 AM

...so many of us making plans trying to please people and/ or fulfill the lusts of the flesh when we know God told us to cancel them plans. Obedience is better than sacrifice and to

hearken is better than the fat of rams. God can see beyond what we can see. Be not deceived.
Feb 19, 2018, 4:07 PM

As people of God, be careful when you say things like, "I hate this situation" or "I really don't like this job, but I have to work it." Be careful complaining and murmuring. Repent. Realize that all things work together for the good of them who love the Lord and those who are called according to His purpose. That job or situation may be all part of the plan that God has for you. That uncomfortable situation or job may be linked to a huge future opportunity or amazing break-through. It's all part of God's plan. Pray and ask God for direction and don't murmur and complain. Makeup your mind to move forward in God's plan with a heart of thanks.
Jan 30, 2017, 7:03 AM

Focus on glory - not the pain.
Jun 6, 2017, 6:45 AM

Sometimes God can deliver us at what we think is the worst time or in a different way than we expected, but all things work together for the good of them who love the Lord and to those called according to His purpose. Father, Let thy will be done.
Sep 21, 2020, 6:32 AM

God-pleaser = Peace
People-pleaser = Stress
Oct 16, 2018, 10:20 PM

Notes from Bible Class:

Real joy comes when you know God has plans of good and not of evil to give you an expected end. Real joy comes when you know God has your back. Real joy comes when you know God cares and wants to reward you and work your situation out. Real joy comes when you CHOOSE IT. Rejoice in the Lord. Don't spend all your energy worried about tomorrow; but, deposit spiritual seeds now for your future. Focus on what really matters and not negativity or distractions. Don't connect happiness to the stuff you have or other people's opinions. Turn away from negative opinions and turn to God. God's opinion is the MAIN one we should really care about. Reference scriptures Psalms 118:24; Phil 1:12-14; Phil 1:15-18; Jere 29:11; Roma 8:28; Phili 4:4

Jan 27, 2019, 3:14 PM

God is the God of order - all in His order and all in His time. Let thy will be done on earth as it is in Heaven.

Oct 6, 2018, 9:22 AM

Congratulations Lady Ervin, Maestro Kenya and King Dan Fauls on placing 1st, 2nd and 3rd place in the Mid-Michigan Gospel Best competition. Thank you to all my loved ones who supported and encouraged me through this. Although I didn't win in this competition, I was obedient to God by singing what His Majesty laid on my heart to sing at this event. Heaven is rejoicing. To God be the glory. I pray that all who participated, listened and was a part of this wonderful gathering are encouraged and strengthened in their relationship with Christ Jesus.

That was the last concert of mine for which my Dad and Big Sister attended while they were on earth. They were rooting for me.

Mar 24, 2019, 7:39 AM

I believe that someone or multiple people prayed to God that I would be at this next local assignment during this time, and why God has allowed me to be temporarily isolated prior to it to gain more strength spiritually.

One of the last assignments I had, the Holy Spirit led me on how to pray and what to do, and some BIG spiritual chains were broken and demonic authorities were removed. Father, let thine will be done.

Oct 5, 2019, 9:12 PM

Dawn Kellum is feeling blessed.

NOTE TO SELF: It is always important for me to remember that whatever areas God has allowed me to minister in - whether as a mother, wife, sister, aunt, cousin, friend; church kitchen, bathroom, nursery and welcome staff, singer, musician, etc. - I must always look up to God for the step-by-step divinely-directed assignment to be accomplished.

Once the specific assignment is accomplished, I look up again to God for the next assignment as my steps are ordered by the sovereign God. It is not in me - a mere human - to direct my own steps when I can't even add 1 second to my own life.

Jul 29, 2019, 11:03 AM

Trust God no matter what you go through
Aug 1, 2020, 10:50 AM

I ask God, "Why me?" Then as He comforts me through words of assurance and hope, I speak through the eyes of faith and say, "Why not Me? God, who is the greatest power, lives within me. Why not show the world how powerful and great God is? Why not show the world that God will never leave you nor forsake you - that He is close to the brokenhearted, faithful and will never refuse a broken and contrite spirit.

He never breaks His promises. He is my Shepherd and knows my name. He is my strength when I'm weak. He keeps me from falling. His love never fails. He took my place on the old rugged cross. He rescues me from evil and leads me beside the quiet streams, restores my soul and leads me in the paths of righteousness for His name's sake. My life and my identity is found in Him.

Dec 10, 2020, 9:20 AM

Romans 8:28 [KJV] "And we know that all things work together for good to them that love God, to them who are the called according to his purpose."

Nov 29, 2013, 8:24 PM

Jesus Christ just let me know that when we can't stand the height of the water any longer, He takes our hand and brings us through the water and says "Come on my beloved one, you will get through no matter what you come up against...just wanted to reassure you that I am with you. You won't drown because you are latched onto me and I am everlasting life and I hold the keys to death, hell and the grave. Death can't take you because I have power over it so when you leave this life you will be with me always..."

May 7, 2013, 10:32 PM

CHAPTER 21

The Bridegroom Cometh

"Wake Up...Don't You Know What Time It is!?"

This is something I say often to my loved ones when it is time for them to go to church, school, work, appointments, etc. and they haven't properly prepared themselves to be at those locations on time.

A similar scenario exists for the coming of the Lord Jesus Christ. Jesus Christ will soon return to earth for those that love and know Him. If you are NOT ready to go with Jesus Christ you WILL remain here on earth. Please read the book of Revelations within the Holy Bible for more about your stay here on earth after the return of our Lord and Savior Jesus Christ.

Why do we as human beings tend to react to situations once they have occurred rather than be proactive and prepare for situations in advance?

For example, I asked a friend of mine a few days ago if they had a plan for retirement on this earth since they are less than 15 years shy of retirement. They had not taken ANY steps to securing their retirement on this earth. This brings to mind the famous quote by Benjamin Franklin — "If you fail to plan, you are planning to fail!"

Likewise, if you have not made yourself ready for the coming of the Lord, you will NOT go with Him when He returns. "If you fail to plan, you are planning to fail!"

The warning of Jesus Christ returning for His saints is NOW and NOT when He actually returns. If you are NOT ready when Jesus Christ returns, you will have NO time to get ready in a moment and a twinkling of an eye (reference I Corinthians 15:52). You will be left behind.

I Died and God Spoke to Me – I was A LUKEWARM CHRISTIAN!

On August 3, 1979, Howard Pittman, a Baptist minister for 35 years, died while on the operating table during surgery and had a near-death experience. After angels showed him the second and third heavens, he was taken before the very throne of God where he was given a message to share with the world.

The following is an excerpt of Chapter 12 – "Wake Up" taken from his booklet, Placebo, which documents his amazing near-death experience.

Chapter 12: Wake Up!

1. For those who CALL themselves Christians, this is the Laodicean Church Age in which we live (Reference Revelations 3:14-22). A high majority of so-called Christians are, in fact, living a deceived life. They talk

Jesus and play church, but do not live it. They claim to be Christians and then live like the devil. They have bought the great lie from satan who tells them that they are alright. He tells them that it is alright to go to church on Sunday and attend mid-week services but as far as the rest of the time is concerned, they are to get all they can out of life. As far as their Christian life is concerned, they believe they are comfortable and have need of nothing and as a result, they are only LUKEWARM Christians if Christians at all.

2. satan is a personal devil. He has a special agenda JUST for you for which the end is eternal death in the torments of HELL and the LAKE OF FIRE.

3. To the whole world, this is Noah's second day. As it was in the days of Noah, so shall it be in the days of the coming of the son of man. Humans took no thought of what Noah was saying nor did humans believe that anything was about to change. Humanity could see the storm clouds over the horizon, but yet did not believe the rain was imminent. Notice the close parallel today. Humanity can see all the signs of the last days, yet humanity does not believe that anything will change. He does not believe in the impending coming of our Lord and he does not prepare to meet God.

4. For those who claim to be Christians, they are supposed to be ambassadors for Christ here on earth. One cannot have any true witness or power in his life unless that one lives his Christian faith at all times, twenty-four hours a day, seven days a week. To be a true Christian one must live it, not just talk it.

To honor God with your lips and not your heart is not acceptable. HONOR GOD WHOLEHEARTEDLY

Those who accept the responsibility of teaching, preaching, or any leadership role have much for which to answer.

God is now in the process of recruiting an army with which God will shake this old world one more time. By working through his soldiers, God will produce great miracles that will shake the established hierarchy of the so-called organized religion that is in this world today. These soldiers that God is now recruiting will demonstrate the power of God to a greater extent than did the disciples in the Pentecostal age. Now the recruitment has begun in earnest because God is about to perform the great miracles through his army that God promised us God would do in the Bible. John the Baptist brought the spirit of Elijah into this world and he did not even know he had it. John denied it, but Jesus confessed that it was so. The purpose of that spirit was to make straight the paths of the coming of the Lord.

23 May, 2014

Message to the Troubled Believer
25 June, 2014
Feeling troubled, hopeless, exhausted as a Christian??
Meriam Ibrahim, 27, of Sudan, refused to renounce her

Christian faith. She was sentenced to death by hanging for apostasy.

John 14:1-3 (AMP) reads the words of our Lord and Savior Jesus Christ as follows:

1 Do not let your hearts be troubled (distressed, agitated). You believe in and adhere to and trust in and rely on God; believe in and adhere to and trust in and rely also on Me.

2 In My Father's house there are many dwelling places (homes). If it were not so, I would have told you; for I am going away to prepare a place for you.

3 And when (if) I go and make ready a place for you, I will come back again and will take you to Myself, that where I am you may be also.

Do you believe this?

Be encouraged by the words of Paul, an apostle of Jesus Christ, a Christian missionary and also one who was imprisoned because he stood for his Christian faith. The following passage written by Paul was taken from 2 Corinthians Chapter 4 (AMP):

2 Corinthians Chapter 4:8 (AMP) We are hedged in (pressed) on every side [troubled and oppressed in every way], but not cramped or crushed; we suffer embarrassments and are perplexed and unable to find a way out, but not driven to despair;

9 We are pursued (persecuted and hard driven), but not deserted [to stand alone]; we are struck down to the ground, but never struck out and destroyed;

10 Always carrying about in the body the liability and ex-

posure to the same putting to death that the Lord Jesus suffered, so that the [[a]resurrection] life of Jesus also may be shown forth by and in our bodies.

13 Yet we have the same spirit of faith as he had who wrote, I have believed, and therefore have I spoken. We too believe, and therefore we speak,

14 Assured that He Who raised up the Lord Jesus will raise us up also with Jesus and bring us [along] with you into His presence.

16 Therefore we do not become discouraged (utterly spiritless, exhausted, and wearied out through fear). Though our outer man is [progressively] decaying and wasting away, yet our inner self is being [progressively] renewed day after day.

17 For our light, momentary affliction (this slight distress of the passing hour) is ever more and more abundantly preparing and producing and achieving for us an everlasting weight of glory [beyond all measure, excessively surpassing all comparisons and all calculations, a vast and transcendent glory and blessedness never to cease!],

Jesus Christ is coming back ANY DAY

In conclusion, fear NOT, be NOT discouraged. Be not weary in well doing. Lean on Jesus Christ. Rely and trust in Jesus Christ. Yes. We all have a cross that we must carry. Yes. We all must suffer. But just know it is ONLY a little while. It may seem long. But it is only a little while.

Exercise the power that Jesus Christ has given you through His blood and His Holy Spirit. Plead His blood and proclaim His promises in your life. Press toward the mark for the prize of the high calling of God in Christ Jesus. Continue to work in the kingdom and tell others about Christ Jesus. Lay hands on the sick and they shall recover. Raise the dead. Cleanse the lepers. Proclaim liberty to the captives. Do this ALL in the name of Jesus Christ. Live your life for Christ Jesus. Take up your cross daily and follow Christ Jesus. Although your outer man may seem to waste away, your inner man is being renewed day by day. Believe in Jesus Christ. Keep the FAITH.

To my sisters and brothers in Christ who are martyrs, Jesus Christ is still Lord. Nothing and none can change that. I will see you in Heaven my brothers and sisters in Christ.

Oct 8, 2015, 6:30 AM

"You will face your greatest opposition when you are closest to your biggest miracle."

Apr 3, 2014, 8:00 PM

No matter what is going on in your life right now, don't lose hope. Your Breakthrough is Coming!

Apr 3, 2014, 7:59 PM

Think like a Champion. Don't Give Up! BELIEVE and KNOW you are a CHAMPION

Apr 3, 2014, 7:58 PM

No matter what you're going through right now, remember that God still reigns on the throne as God and God alone.

God is WITH you AND trouble doesn't last always. Endure hardness as a good soldier of Christ Jesus. Be Encouraged.

May 29, 2014, 6:17 AM

Dawn Kellum was traveling to Lansing, Michigan.

..heading to church for youth service- Hebrews 10:25 (GW) We should not stop gathering together with other believers, as some of you are doing. Instead, we must continue to encourage each other even more as we see the day of the Lord coming.

Apr 27, 2014, 5:28 PM

Philosophies of this kingdom don't create overcomers of this same kingdom. Only the philosophies, strategies and tactics from another kingdom create overcomers on this kingdom on earth. Quit looking around you for the answers we need today. Look up!

May 8, 2015, 6:49 AM

At the end of a race you don't play around you GET SERIOUS. Further, in the END time that we are in NOW, DON'T play around. It's time to GET SERIOUS about Jesus Christ. Don't be deceived. Jesus Christ's return for those who love and know Him is right upon us. It's IMMINENT. If you're not ready, get ready and stay on fire for God. Welcome Him and His word into EVERY area of your life. No more LUKEWARM. Stay on fire and passionate about the kingdom of God.

Jul 21, 2014, 11:10 PM

...fear NOT and be NOT discouraged. Be not weary in well doing. Lean on Jesus Christ. Rely and trust in Jesus Christ. Yes. We all have a cross that we must carry. Yes. We all must suffer. But just know it is ONLY a little while. It may seem long, but it is only a little while.

Jul 18, 2014, 7:36 AM

Hold on. Don't give up. You will reap if you faint not. Every storm runs out of rain. Trust that God will see you through. [HUGS]

Aug 11, 2014, 9:44 PM

Dawn Kellum updated her status.

Thank you Jesus for the reminder from 1 Peter 5:8 (AMP) to be well balanced (temperate, sober of mind), be vigilant and cautious at all times; for that enemy of yours, the devil, roams around like a lion roaring [in fierce hunger], seeking someone to seize upon and devour.

Dec 5, 2014, 6:41 AM

Remember that the fight is fixed. In the end, we, the over-comers through Jesus Christ, win!

Jan 5, 2015, 10:03 PM

Keep your head up
Cause a new day will come
And look towards [GOD]
Even when the darkness shall come

Jan 24, 2015, 9:14 PM

Dawn Kellum is feeling sad.

Meditating. We enter life like we enter a department store. We all enter through the same door. What we do in that department store will determine which door we exit. The door we entered is not the same door we exit and everyone has to check out. Are we ready for check out? Which door will we exit once we check out?

Mar 1, 2015, 12:21 AM

....Serving notice to my enemies that quitting is NOT an option. It's not over until my God says it's over. My God rules in and about me and has the Last Say!

May 6, 2015, 6:49 AM

Dawn Kellum updated her status.

Fear not. There are more of us than it is of our enemies. We are more than able. The gates of hell shall not prevail against the kingdom of God represented on earth.

Apr 22, 2015, 7:04 AM

I have so much peace now that I'm off my agenda and on Christ' agenda. The whole world's in chaos but Christ Jesus is my peace. Period.

Apr 24, 2015, 6:56 AM

Dawn Kellum is feeling loved.

1 Peter 4:14 (NLT) If you are insulted because you bear the name of Christ, you will be blessed, for the glorious Spirit of God rests upon you. 15 If you suffer, however, it must not

be for murder, stealing, making trouble, or prying into other people's affairs.

Jun 16, 2015, 6:33 AM

The trumpet is about to sound signifying our Messiah's return. Those who are living for Him long for this day and will see it as a wonderful time of joy and triumph, but those who are not in right-standing with God will experience dread and destruction.

Sep 2, 2015, 7:18 AM

Dawn Kellum is feeling focused.

Since we are surrounded by so many examples of faith, we must get rid of everything that slows us down, especially sin that distracts us. We must run the race that lies ahead of us and never give up. Hebrews 12:1 (GW)

Nov 13, 2015, 11:01 AM

Don't wait until the battle is over. Shout now. Praise God even through the test. This proves that you trust Him for a victorious outcome. Hallelujah! ..."we KNOW that God causes everything to work together[a] for the good of those who LOVE GOD and are called according to HIS purpose for them." Rom. 8:28 [NLT]

Apr 26, 2016, 6:00 AM

God is teaching me to be flexible and to wear this world as a loose garment. Loose garments are more comfortable and permit lots of movement and flexibility.

FYI. Jonah wore the world as a tight garment, lots of ego, lots of attachment, etc.

Feb 24, 2016, 5:41 AM

Luke 22:32 (ESV) But I have prayed for you that your faith may not fail. And when you have turned again, strengthen your brothers."

Apr 3, 2016, 7:47 AM

Luke 21:25 And there shall be signs in the sun, and in the moon, and in the stars; and upon the earth distress of nations, with perplexity; the sea and the waves roaring;

26 Men's hearts failing them for fear, and for looking after those things which are coming on the earth: for the powers of heaven shall be shaken.

27 And then shall they see the Son of man coming in a cloud with power and great glory.

28 And when these things begin to come to pass, then look up, and lift up your heads; for your redemption draweth nigh.

Sep 7, 2017, 6:56 PM

Jesus Christ is saying....

Those who minister through Jesus Christ must love, know & exalt Him in every aspect, be unselfish, patient, loving, anointed by the Holy Spirit, stay humble, not filled with pride, not greedy for self-attention or worldly power and must live the life of a believer who has a 1 on 1 relationship with Christ Jesus. Jesus said, "If I be lifted up from the earth I will draw ALL men unto me - not YOU be lifted up." Why exalt flesh which has boundaries? Pride goeth before destruction and a haughty spirit before a fall.

Jun 3, 2016, 6:33 AM

Wear this world as a loose garment. My Daddy's pastor, Pastor Collins of CSGBT, used to say "Don't even put it on."

Nov 11, 2016, 6:24 AM

Remember that when you're building for the kingdom of God, demonic spirits are always trying to dig up holes around you to bury, overwhelm and overcome all your efforts; but, know that the gates of hell shall not prevail against that work and God has not forgotten your labor of love. Be Encouraged.

Mar 5, 2018, 7:11 AM

Make the journey matter so that once you get to your destination you have no regrets.

Jun 7, 2017, 7:01 AM

Guard your heart and your mind. God is more than the world against you. He is the light that shines from within and the outside in piercing darkness and evil. He is the Father of lights. He always does what He promises. No weapon formed against me shall prosper. Seek to please God in all you do and He will bring victory over enemies and make your enemies your footstool.

The wicked shall not reign or have control over those who love and know God – no matter what it looks like. He will not allow any other god to be god over you. None can snatch you from God's hands. Let Jesus Christ be the LORD of your life. Satan, our Lord Jesus Christ doth rebuke you. Nothing and no one can keep the children of God from the love of God through Christ Jesus.

God's love is the only love that never fails. Please Him first. Put God first. Pray for those who hatefully use you and tell lies about you. Become the love of God. Forgive. Worship God and praise God for revealing and exposing their ungodly intent even though you hurt.

People are fickle but God is faithful as promised. He is the Amazing God. What you do for Christ Jesus is what eternally matters. Be not weary in well doing for you shall reap if you faint not.

Oct 9, 2017, 9:14 PM

Jesus loves us. What does Jesus think of our lifestyles? Are we serving Jesus? Don't be a hypocrite. Lucifer was cast out of heaven because he mixed the worship of God with his own agenda. He desired to be lifted up and famous while trying to lead the worship of God. This didn't work in that realm and it definitely does not work in our realm. When performers embrace the sin filled lyrics and music of the world's recording artists, they are promoting the very thing that Christ is against.

We understand that we all sin and fall short, but lifestyle practicing of sin is another issue. An artist who promotes lewd sexual acts, vulgar language, threesomes, degenerative sexual behavior, multiple sex partners, and multiple personality disorders (not referring to dissociative identity disorder – a diagnosed mental illness) needs to be helped and not promoted by the church. Gospel artists are so excited to work with the enemy's agents that they will skip right over that person's need of repentance just to do a song with them which validates their current behavior. Those evil spirits will leap on you instead and leave you and others following you naked, UNCOVERED and wounded. This is because of the perversion and because your lives are not yielding to Christ Jesus.

Apr 14, 2018, 7:41 AM

'Taint no jellyback soldiers in 'dis army. Jesus Christ IS your backbone when He is your master and housekeeper. He and His Father have come to dine with you. Gird up the loins of your mind. Be sober and watchful. The hero lies in you. Jesus Christ lives in you. Stand upright and fight the good fight using spiritual weapons - not carnal ones. Fight with the weapons given by the most high God. Be strong in the Lord and in the power of His might.

Dec 17, 2017, 7:19 AM

I want to fight! I don't want comfort! I don't want ease in Zion! Because the kingdom of God is built not by those who rest easily in Zion, but by those who go out into the streets and fight. And the weapons of our warfare are not carnal. They are mighty. Examples include intercessory prayer, the proclamation of the Gospel, sacrificial love and more.

Oct 15, 2020, 10:48 PM

...and the world is really shaking now...Don't get distracted. Stay focused. Jesus is about to take the "salt" out the earth.

Jun 23, 2020, 7:47 AM

...that time when turmoil kept coming and some repented while others became more and more wicked. Remember Moses and Pharoah? Remember Jonah? Remember King Nebuchadnezzar?

Mar 25, 2020, 5:58 PM

No man having put his hand to the plough and looking back is fit for the Kingdom of Heaven. -Reference Luke 9:62

Oct 23, 2018, 7:43 AM

Jesus Christ is soon to return. When you hear about wars and rumors of wars, look up! Your redemption is near. They that endure to the end, the same shall be saved

Apr 14, 2018, 10:42 AM

...reflecting on yesterday's noonday meditation/bible study - But as it is written, Eye hath not seen, nor ear heard, neither have entered into the heart of man, the things which God hath prepared for them that love Him.

I consider our present sufferings insignificant compared to the glory that will soon be revealed to us.

Jul 26, 2018, 7:00 AM

...a sermon takeaway from what the Pastor taught at this week's noonday bible class at the Breadhouse - Servants of the kingdom of God should be serving the kingdom menu. Don't hijack the kingdom's message for your own agenda or for pride. God knows your thoughts afar off and the intentions of your heart.

Apr 29, 2018, 8:30 AM

Be ready. Stay ready. Do not be deceived. Repent now while the Kingdom of Heaven is at hand. Keep a repentant heart. Jesus Christ is returning in the Rapture as the Bible affirms. Everything that is supposed to have happened before the Rapture has already happened. I pray we will all be ready.

Dec 7, 2018, 6:01 AM

Happy Birthday Dr. Martin Luther King Jr. "We've got some difficult days ahead," Martin Luther King, Jr., told an overflowing crowd in Memphis, Tennessee, on 3 April 1968, where the city's sanitation workers were striking. "But it really doesn't matter with me now, because I've been to the mountaintop ... I've seen the Promised Land. I may not get there with you. But I want you to know tonight, that we, as a people, will get to the Promised Land" Less than 24 hours after these prophetic words, King was assassinated by James Earl Ray.

In a prophetic finale to his speech, King revealed that he

was not afraid to die: "Like anybody, I would like to live a long life—longevity has its place. But I'm not concerned about that now. I just want to do God's will.... And so I'm happy tonight; I'm not worried about anything; I'm not fearing any man. Mine eyes have seen the glory of the coming of the Lord."

Follow peace with all mankind as much as possible. Without holiness we shall not see the Lord's face in peace. Pray for all people AND your enemies and those who use you hatefully and have your worst interest at heart. God does not like how we treat each other wrong. We are to show the love of Christ Jesus to everybody. Thou shalt love the Lord thy God with all thy heart, soul and mind AND love thy neighbor as thyself. We are not to be judgmental but to be loving at all times. We are to take on the attributes of God's Holy Spirit. Receive it! We are to show kindness to people and be merciful. God had mercy on us so we should have mercy on others. God loved us first so we should love each other. We as Christians should not be so quick to condemn other people but to love them and show them the love of Jesus Christ.

People are using the gifts and talents that God has given them to serve up the kingdom of darkness' menu or agenda rather than the kingdom of God's menu or agenda. Be a true servant of the kingdom of God. Love one another as Christ Jesus loved you. The way that Jesus taught us how to treat people is the right way.

January 15, 2020

Words that help me stay focused (notes taken from Bible Study):

-Building with the right material is important.

-Have solid anchors in your building.

-Don't build based off of popularity or being a celebrity; but, on a solid foundation.

-The enemy will try to get you distracted and slip you a "mickey" to steal your hope, faith or love; however, in tough times and/or in the midst of distractions, trust God and stand on His word.

-Resist the enemy with the word of God and he will flee.

-Love God so much where there is no room for any other god in your life.

-Our love for God drives everything else in our lives.

-What areas in our lives has the love for God been neglected?-1st Commandment by God - "..love the LORD thy God with all thine heart, and with all thy soul, and with all thy might."

- Have Heart love for God. Have Mind love for God. Have Soul love for God. Have Strength love for God.

Jun 14, 2019, 12:51 PM

LOVE GOD WITH ALL YOUR HEART, SOUL, MIND AND STRENGTH

The first and greatest commandment by God is LOVE THE LORD YOUR GOD WITH ALL YOUR HEART, AND WITH ALL YOUR SOUL, AND WITH ALL YOUR MIND, AND WITH ALL YOUR STRENGTH.

We are in the last days. Jesus Christ is coming back from Heaven to this earth for those who love and know Him. It is time to serve God with all of our heart, mind, soul AND strength. He wants to know those who have accepted Him as Lord of their lives AND truly love Him with all their heart, mind, soul and strength.

It is going to get rough out here trying to live holy for Jesus Christ but who will stay on fire for God? will you just honor God with your lips?? Or will you honor Him with your heart also?

Here is another thing to remember. Don't let ANY-THING or ANYONE separate you from the love of Christ Jesus. Don't let ANYTHING or ANYONE separate your good relationship with God. Don't allow anyone or anything to come between you and your God.

Romans 8:35 says Who shall separate us from the love of Christ? shall tribulation, or distress, or persecution, or famine, or nakedness, or peril, or sword? 36 As it is written, For thy sake we are killed all the day long; we are accounted as sheep for the slaughter. 37 Nay, in all these things we are more than conquerors through him that loved us. 38 For I am persuaded, that neither death, nor life, nor angels, nor principalities, nor powers, nor things present, nor things to come, 39 Nor height, nor depth, nor any other creature, shall be able to separate us from the love of God, which is in Christ Jesus our Lord.

God wants us to hold fast to Him. He wants us to be on fire for Him.

Revelations 3:15 says I know thy works, that thou art neither cold nor hot: I would thou wert cold or hot. 16 So then because thou art lukewarm, and neither cold nor hot, I will spue thee out of my mouth.

We must be HOT or on fire for God - That means serving and loving Him with all our heart soul mind and strength ..not being lukewarm. Seek God and Love God with all your heart, mind, soul and strength.

There is a song called "Send the Fire" by William Booth who started the Salvation Army

Here are some of the words:

God of Elijah, hear our cry: Send the fire, send the fire, send the fire! To make us fit to live or die, Send the fire, send the fire, send the fire! To burn up every trace of sin, To bring the light and glory in, The revolution now begin, Send the fire, send the fire, send the fire!

We need to say, "I must know you God. I'm desperate for you. I need you. I'm hungry for you. You're the only one that really truly matters God. There is nothing better than you God."

You ask How can I love God with all my heart, mind, soul and strength? You can only truly love God with all your heart, mind, soul and strength by receiving Jesus Christ as Lord of your life because Christ must be in you for you to please God and love God with all your heart, mind, soul and strength.

Allow Jesus Christ to be Lord of your life now. He loves you more than you could ever imagine. How can I Allow Jesus Christ to be Lord of my life? Romans 10:9 – 10 says if thou shalt confess with thy mouth the Lord Jesus, and shalt believe in thine heart that God hath raised him from the dead, thou shalt be saved.....and with the mouth confession is made unto salvation.

Accept Jesus Christ as Lord and Savior of your life. If you need Jesus and want a personal relationship with Him, pray this very simple prayer out loud: "Father God, I love you. I believe in you. I need you. I'm sorry for my sins. Sorry about the way I've lived. Sorry for shutting You out. I want You in my life. I surrender. I yield. I receive Jesus Christ as my Savior and my Lord. I believe He died for me. He rose from the dead. He's alive today. Come into me. Take me just the way I am. Now make me everything You want me to be. I believe I'm saved. I'm on my way to heaven, and I'm going to enjoy the trip. Amen."

Now that you have received Jesus Christ as Lord and Savior of your life, publicly acknowledge the death, burial and resurrection of Jesus Christ by being water-baptized in the name of Jesus Christ and also receive the Holy Spirit that is evidenced by speaking in tongues according to Acts Chapter 2.

Now when you receive the Holy Ghost aka the Holy Spirit, according to Luke 3:16, that Holy Spirit comes with fire power to help you live right for God and stay on fire for God.

Don't let anything or anyone separate you from the love of God through Christ Jesus. Go to church. Hear and Do the word of God. Go hard after Jesus. Don't be lukewarm. Be real with God. He knows your shortcomings. He knows your ups and downs. Confess your issues to Him. He is ready and willing to help you. Let Him be Lord of your life today and love God with all your heart, mind, soul and strength. In the midst of turmoil, hold onto God and seek Him while He may be found. Call to Him while He is near and while you have a chance to turn unto Him. Repent of your sins and accept our Lord and Savior Jesus Christ as your Savior. He will be your comfort in sorrow, your healer through the pain and more. Worship Him in spirit and in truth; from the heart. Love the Lord your God with all your heart, mind, soul and strength.

Thank you for listening. May the grace of God be with you in Jesus name.

28 July, 2016

...when your 9 year old daughter leaves Children's' Church and preaches almost the entire way home about repentance and saying words like, "Mommy, even CHRISTIANS won't go up in the Rapture if they have not repented. Only a few will go to Heaven. All Christians won't go to Heaven Mommy. We need to pray and ask God to forgive us for all our sins. If someone has a half-naked picture in their room, that is sin Mommy because they are a pervert. Mommy, we prayed and asked God to forgive us of our sins..." Wheeeeeew..

Jul 7, 2019, 2:09 PM

...laying aside every weight in pursuit of God.

Feb 13, 2020, 9:29 AM

As some of the Israelites didn't make it to the Promised Land, some of us will never see New Jerusalem.

Oct 4, 2019, 8:28 PM

It doesn't matter who betrayed you or lied on you. Don't turn your back on God. Run to Him and not away from Him. At times, God has to show us the ugly truth about situations and people; but, don't run away from Him because He exposed some stuff. Stay in God. Let Him comfort and enlighten you. Be engulfed in truth.

Aug 22, 2019, 4:27 PM

Our God-given gifts and/or God's anointing at work in our lives to perform miracles and more does NOT give us permission to live any kind of life we want or treat people any kind of way. Many of us will never see New Jerusalem for these very reasons. Don't rejoice because you are anointed or have a gift, rejoice because your name is written in the Lamb's Book of Life. If your name is not written there, you will be cast into the Lake of Fire – the 2nd death.

Nov 23, 2019, 7:35 AM

Although my Heavenly Father leads and guides me with His Holy Spirit, I am also SO very grateful for my godly mentors who delight in the laws of God and constantly seek the heart of God in a society where good morale, patience and other good fruits are not popular. Additionally, mentors are enthusiastic about their role, should fit you, are active listeners, know how to provide feedback, treats others respectfully, are experts in their field, value learning and encourages you to step out of your comfort zone.

Jan 13, 2020, 10:32 AM

Global epidemic disease or pestilence was predicted many years ago by Jesus Christ, the son of God, not to SCARE us but to PREPARE us for what is to come after. Our physical health is important, but our spiritual health is more important. We all need salvation through Jesus Christ.

Mar 10, 2020, 10:15 PM

If it draws you away from serving God, let it go
Feb 18, 2020, 6:00 AM

I know you're tempted, but don't fall into the traps of the enemy. God will take care of you.

Mar 17, 2020, 7:59 AM

I shared this from another source. During this season during the Pandemic, we should not be watching porn, entertaining witchcraft and taking heed to seducing spirits and doctrines of devils in the supposed quiet areas of our homes that have turned into demonic altars while keeping many of us bound emotionally, mentally and spiritually. A lot of people are getting STDs (Spiritually Transmitted Demons) in this season. Repent. Jesus loves you.

May 1, 2020, 10:23 AM

I remember my Daddy Bishop Nathaniel Edwards, Sr. said that, in regards to the ministry of the gospel of the Jesus Christ, "If the people sent you, the people will also send you back. When God sends you, the people can't send you back."

Jun 15, 2020, 3:41 PM

Get in Position to be used by the Lord.
Jun 17, 2020, 9:24 PM

Move forward.
Jun 18, 2020, 5:01 AM

Depart from me you worker of iniquity. I never knew you.
Be cast into outer darkness.
Jul 23, 2020, 6:42 AM

Word from Heaven: Don't put your God-Given gifts and talents on the shelf in this season. Use them.
Jul 8, 2020, 7:21 AM

Praise God. At least 3 people gave their lives to the Lord Jesus during the recent street revival at ATOP Church a few days ago. Many received the message of hope. Many people were also watching and some were filming. Some were also parked in surrounding parking lots. Others stopped their vehicles in the street, were pulling up in their cars and many physically there with us in the parking lot. People were still coming even after it was over. To God be the glory.
Aug 8, 2020, 10:29 PM

It's too late for burn out. Preach Pastor Nathaniel Edwards, Jr.

Jul 14, 2020, 6:42 AM

Be careful of hidden agendas that are against God.

Aug 31, 2020, 3:11 PM

You can make your greatest impact in the kingdom of Christ Jesus by having His love - not selfish with hidden ungodly agendas.

Oct 18, 2020, 8:48 AM

The fields are white already but the laborers are few.

Aug 10, 2020, 6:23 PM

Take It to the Streets. All glory to God. Use me Lord for your service.

Aug 11, 2020, 5:35 AM

Don't profess the narrow way and live the broad way.

Oct 15, 2020, 10:43 PM

Be Encouraged to do more for Christ Jesus. Don't let the devil discourage you. satan knows that you now belong to JESUS forever and that he can NEVER get you back unless you surrender to him - so since he can't STOP you from being a CHRISTIAN, the next best thing he tries to do is to try to stop you from being an ACTIVE Christian. He'll try to make you a DEAD Christian, instead of a real LIVE one! He'll fight and try to stop you from SERVING the Lord, and defeat you from being a good sample to win OTHERS, because he's afraid that he might lose others from his clutches because of YOU!

Mar 16, 2014, 8:07 AM

Dawn Kellum is feeling hopeful.

Some people say church is like a hospital in regards to healing. If hospital doctors and nurses cannot discriminate on who they help to heal, then why do church ministers discriminate on who they help to heal?

Oct 31, 2020, 1:48 PM

If you give chrysanthemum seeds to a planter to grow chrysanthemums and they don't know how to grow them, should the planter reject them to be, hopefully and possibly, planted in another garden?

A planter researches seeds and examines the why, what, how, when, where and more about seeds.

How long will the seed remain a seed before it's planted in the right garden and grows to strengthen, change form and flourish? The seed is waiting to be planted. How does your plant grow? How does your garden grow?

Nov 1, 2020, 7:58 AM

"Jesus is coming back y'all. People having dreams about the rapture, saved and unsaved, God showing people signs..Saints are leaving out of here by the numbers...come in before it's too late. No time for bad attitudes, temper tantrums, rebelliousness, sneaky plots or backsliding...it's time to get ready y'all!!!!!!!! When Jesus comes, what will you be doing? People think Holiness is so lame...Naw, Holiness is that deal, it gets you into the divine presence of God. It's the safest place to be. Time to choose home. You want Heaven or do you want Hell?" - Posted by Ashley Starks Morris

Feb 4, 2014, 5:14 AM

Jesus Christ just told me through the Holy Spirit "Whatever the devil stole from you, You WILL get it back. Believe, rely and trust in Me." Friends and family, we got to hang in there. We got some rough ridin' now and ahead. If your soul is not anchored in Jesus Christ you will give up and turn BACK to the things of this world. Trust in Jesus Christ to the E N D.

He is R E A L!

Sep 4, 2013, 6:33 PM

Dawn Kellum shared a post to the group: CHURCH FOLKS

Please. Come back. Your heavenly Father wants you to return home. There are beasts and other orders that will be unleashed upon the earth after the saints are taken out of the earth in the rapture. Those things that will be unleashed will not allow you to have any peace. Please just come home. Let the pride and ego go.

Oct 25, 2020, 6:41 AM

IN CONCLUSION

It is important, as an ambassador of Christ Jesus' kingdom, to wear this world as a loose garment and, while walking through "Babylon" sharing the good news of the gospel, to not get consumed by the lust of the eye, the lust of the flesh or the pride of life. STAY FOCUSED MY SISTERS AND BROTHERS. God is with you.

Be of good courage, cheer, boldness and confidence and God shall strengthen thee. David also said to Solomon his son, Be strong and courageous and do the work. Do not be afraid or discouraged for the LORD God my God is with you. He will not fail you or forsake you until all the work for the service of the temple of the LORD is finished. (1 Chronicles 28:20) Therefore, my dear brothers and sisters, stand firm. Let nothing move you. Always give yourselves fully to the work of the Lord, because you know that your labor in the Lord is not in vain. (1 Corinthians 15:58)

Do not be afraid or terrified because of them for the LORD your God goes with you; he will never leave you nor forsake you. Then Moses summoned Joshua and said to him in the presence of all Israel, The LORD himself goes before you and will be with you; he will never leave you nor forsake you. Do not be afraid; do not be discouraged. (Deuteronomy 31:6-8)

Finally, be strong in the Lord and in his mighty power. (Ephesians 6:10) Do not be afraid; you will not be put to shame. Do not fear disgrace; you will not be humiliated. You will forget the shame of your youth and remember no more the reproach of your widowhood. (Isaiah 54:4)

Peace I leave with you; my peace I give you. I do not give to you as the world gives. Do not let your hearts be troubled and do not be afraid. (John 14:27)

The LORD is my light and my salvation— whom shall I fear? The LORD is the stronghold of my life— of whom shall I be afraid? (Psalm 27:1)

Endtime Deception.

A great point of biblical reference is from Genesis Chapter 3 when Eve was deceived by the Serpent aka satan aka the devil aka the master deceiver aka the father of lies.

Genesis 3:1-6 (AMP) Now the serpent was more crafty (subtle, skilled in deceit) than any living creature of the field which the Lord God had made. And the serpent (Satan) said to the woman, "Can it really be that God has said, 'You shall not eat from any tree of the garden'?" 2 And the woman said to the serpent, "We may eat fruit from the trees of the garden, 3 except the fruit from the tree which is in the middle of the garden. God said, 'You shall not eat from it nor touch it, otherwise you will die.'" 4 But the serpent said to the woman, "You certainly will not die! 5 For God knows that on the day you eat from it your eyes will be opened [that is, you will have greater awareness], and you will be like God, knowing [the difference between] good and evil." 6 And when the woman saw that the tree was good for food, and that it was delightful to look at, and a tree to be desired in order to make one wise and insightful, she took some of its fruit and ate it; and she also gave some to her husband [c]with her, and he ate.

Question. Why did the devil go to Eve rather than Adam?

Answer. Understand that God gave the commandment to Adam. The devil wanted Eve to no longer trust her source of truth. The devil went to the woman so she would no longer trust the authority of the man - her husband Adam. Could she have been approached because of her emotional nature or that she possibly considered that her husband was somehow hiding something from her?

As long as you continue to question your source of truth as a believer in Christ Jesus, you are at RISK OF BEING DECEIVED by the father of lies - satan! The devil's job is to change the truth into a lie and make you believe that the truth you have received is not the "whole" truth.

"This ploy of the enemy is to plant a seed of doubt to make you question what you know and make you feel you have been held back or deprived of the real truth because of an ulterior motive." - ex Ministries, 2021

Consider the following scripture. St. John 8:32 "And ye shall know the truth, and the truth shall make you free. "If you know and experience the truth, you will not be deceived. Jesus Christ is the way, the truth and the life. If you know and experience Jesus Christ, who is truth, and do not question His truth, you will not be deceived by the father of deceit - the devil.

Consider the following scripture. Hosea 4:6 "My people are destroyed for lack of knowledge: because thou hast rejected knowledge, I will also reject thee, that thou shalt be no priest to me: seeing thou hast forgotten the law of thy God, I will also forget thy children."

Be careful going on time-consuming "quests for knowledge" when you should be rather surrendering to God and trusting His word and knowing and experiencing the truth - who is Jesus Christ. Why question the truth you have already received and experienced through your relationship with Jesus Christ? Could Eve have easily looked around her and been grateful for what she had already? Why did she not stand on God's word and hold God's word as the only source of truth? Jesus is not holding you back from the truth because He is the truth you should seek and experience. He is the way. He is the life you seek. Seek Him. Don't allow the devil to plant a seed of doubt to the truth you KNOW and have EXPERIENCED. Be not deceived brothers and sisters.

Consider the following scriptures:

Romans 3:4 God forbid: yea, let God be true, but every man a liar; as it is written, That thou mightest be justified in thy sayings, and mightest overcome when thou art judged.

Psalm 100:5 For the LORD is good; his mercy is everlasting; and his truth endureth to all generations.

THANK YOU

I am grateful that you took the time to read this book. I pray that you are encouraged and ever- inspired to focus on God and allow His Holy Spirit to lead, guide, comfort, reveal and so much more!

You may also read more inspiring articles and connect with me on my websites:
www.dawnkellum.com or www.womenunspotted.com

2 Corinthians 13:14 Now may the grace of God, the love of Jesus, and the sweet communion of the Holy Spirit, rest, rule, and abide now, henceforth and forevermore. Amen.